Zendesk for Customer Service Agents

How to solve tickets in Zendesk Support

Nils Rebehn

Other Works[1]

Online Courses

- Zendesk for Agents
- Zendesk for Admins

Zendesk Resources

- Toolbox for Zendesk
- Blog and Newsletter

---

[1]All courses and resources can be found at www.nilsrebehn.com/my-zendesk-resources

Colophon

Publisher: Independent Publishing Network.
Publication date: 2021-06
ISBN: 978-1-80049-641-5

Author: Nils Rebehn
Editor: Anton de Young
Please direct all enquiries to the author via
www.NilsRebehn.com.

Guidoo Services™ is a trademark of Guidoo Services Limited, UK.

Zendesk™ and all its products, logos, icons, and other visuals or sounds are protected by copyright and or trademark of Zendesk Inc. US.

Dedication

This is for my fiancé and our future.
This is for my parents, to make them proud.

🌳 I'll dedicate (donate) one tree for every sold ebook or printed book.

🧱 I'll donate one brick to build schools for every sold ebook or printed book.

About the author

Nils worked at Zendesk for 5 years as part of their Professional Services and Customer Success team. He founded Guidoo Services, an official Zendesk Partner, to help companies get the most out of Zendesk.

He and his team successfully implemented Zendesk for hundreds of companies, both large and small. Over the years, Nils trained thousands on using and setting up Zendesk.

Outside of customer service, he is an entrepreneur and environmentalist.

You can find him on LinkedIn[2] and via his website[3].

Updates to this book

Get updates and errata on this book. I was as thorough as possible, but there might be some mistakes in this book that I need to correct later on.

Also, I plan to update this book when Zendesk introduces changes to the agent experience. Sign up for updates to this book[4].

---

[2] www.linkedin.com/in/nrebehn/
[3] www.nilsrebehn.com/
[4] www.nilsrebehn.com/books-zendesk-for-agents-updates

Table Of Contents

All exercises

Introduction

Chapters in this section:

- Is this book for you?
- What you'll learn
- How to use this book
- What is Zendesk?
- What you'll need

Is this book for you?

If you are new to Zendesk and don't know where to start, this book is for you. It's written for:

- **Beginners**: everyone new to the Zendesk platform
- People who want to learn **how to work with tickets**
- **Customer service** representatives who need Zendesk for their job
- IT administrators who need to improve the **agent experience**
- **Managers** who want to understand the agent's perspective
- Everyone who has used another ticketing system before
- Learners that want everything in one place
- People who prefer text over video

This book is for everyone that is not familiar with Zendesk or doesn't know how to use it. It will teach you the basics of using it for customer service or Customer Support (CS for short). You'll learn how to answer people's questions and solve tickets in the process.

It doesn't matter if your job title is Customer Service Agent, CS Representative, CS Advocate, "Customer Happiness

Consultant", or something else. There are many job titles in the customer service space. To put it in other words: you want to read this book if you work in a CS team and use Zendesk to support customers.

Knowing how to use Zendesk will help you to secure a job in the customer service industry because Zendesk is a market leader in this segment. If you are just beginning your career in CS with Zendesk, or even if you have worked with other platforms but not Zendesk yet, this book is the best starting point!

Are you running your own business? Are you considering Zendesk for your inbound customer communication? If so, this book will help you determine if Zendesk is the Customer Support platform you need.

Practical exercises

Experience Zendesk for Agents firsthand in your own trial account. Practical exercises are included in the sections of this book. I recommend reading the book chapter by chapter. You can then either follow these exercises in the applicable part of the book or do them all in one go at the end.

Topics we won't cover

This book is focused on using Zendesk from the perspective of a customer service employee, whose job it is to reply to customers, respond to questions, or assist them with their queries.

If you want to learn about Zendesk administration or how to set up Zendesk for your business, department, or team, I can recommend other resources such as books or online training courses[5].

This book covers tickets that come in via email, website support request forms, or a help centre. It doesn't cover providing support via chat, phone, or instant messaging. Although, many of the principles of working with tickets are the same and are therefore transferable.

Have you already worked with Zendesk for a couple of months? Do you know how to update and solve tickets already? If so, you might want to skip the first half and go directly to the sections on *Customising Zendesk for you*, *Productivity tips*, and the *Day In The Life Of An Agent*.

---

[5] www.nilsrebehn.com/my-zendesk-courses

What you'll learn

This book is a great starting point for learning Zendesk from the ground up, from the Agent's perspective. It teaches you how to use the Zendesk platform and what you need to know to help customers.

The official Zendesk documentation is detailed and useful and can help with specific topics and questions; however, it's easy to get lost after reading a handful of articles. This book instead takes you on a journey from the beginning to a clear and defined goal; teaching you everything you need to know to use Zendesk as an Agent[6], and in an order that makes sense and builds on what you learn at each step.

You will learn:

- Zendesk basics and the user interface
- What tickets are and where they come from
- How to work with tickets and respond to customers
- How to solve email tickets
- Zendesk productivity tips and best practices

---

[6] See glossary on page 242

By going through this book, chapter by chapter, you will experience what a day in an Agent's life can look like and see how everything you learn here comes together. You can learn at your own pace, whenever you want, and you will have plenty of opportunities to get hands-on with practical exercises as well.

How to use this book

You can read the book from front to back to learn everything in an order that makes sense for beginners. It's arranged so that the topics and your learning stack up like building blocks.

If you are in a rush, feel free to skip ahead—but I recommend reading the first two sections as they lay the foundation for everything that follows. They are easy to read, take little time, but are essential for understanding the basics. After you've read them, you can read and make sense of any other part of the book.

Tip: There will be times when something in Zendesk is not obvious or has a hidden functionality, and there might be a range of good options to choose from or a best way of doing something. On those occasions, I will provide you with a recommendation that is based on my experience as a consultant and trainer, and also on customer service best practices.

I highlight these as tips, which you'll see clearly marked with the word **Tip** in bold font followed by my advice.

Follow along with step-by-step exercises

You will find many chapters that invite you to follow along with practical exercises that you can do on your own. These are step-by-step exercises that you can do if you want to get hands-on with the Zendesk platform, using your own account. If you don't have access to a Zendesk account, I provide instructions for getting your free trial account.

It's not necessary to do these exercises as you're reading the chapters. Instead, you can skip over them, read on, and do them later. Also, they are not essential for your learning. You can consume the entire book and learn everything you need to know without doing the exercises. Nonetheless, it will be helpful for you to experience the platform firsthand and doing these exercises reinforce what you are reading.

The exercises are clearly marked in chapters throughout the sections of this book. You'll see a heading with the name of the exercise and an estimate of how much time it will take to follow along. You can find the complete list of exercises in the table of contents[7].

---

[7] See Table Of Contents on page 11

Glossary and bibliography

At the end of the book, you'll find a glossary[8] that will help you with customer service terms that you may not already be familiar with.

The bibliography[9] is a list of the external sources of information that are mentioned in this book. You can use it to dive deeper into specific topics.

---

[8] See glossary on page 242
[9] See bibliography on page 246

What is Zendesk?

Ask five different people in the customer service industry what Zendesk is and you'll get five different answers—and that includes people that work at Zendesk.

I worked at Zendesk for five years, and I don't have the perfect one-liner to summarise it either. This is partly because it has evolved a lot over time. It's also because it can serve various purposes in different companies.

Here's my personal explanation, with relevant context.

Zendesk is a cloud-based (SaaS) customer service platform. It's often referred to as a Customer Relationship Management (CRM) system, while others describe it as a simple ticketing system. Neither quite captures it.

A classic CRM usually holds lots of customer information. It contains contact details like addresses, phone numbers, and business interactions such as quotes and orders. The emphasis for most CRM systems is on **Customer Management**, not the relationship part.

In contrast, Zendesk is excellent for managing the **Relationship** with your customers—unlike a classic CRM. By that I mean the interactions your business has with its customers. The focus is not so much on the contact data and orders. With Zendesk, it's about the conversations a company has with their customers.

And yet, Zendesk is not a simple ticketing system either—that's not the complete story. Yes, it captures the customer communication as tickets, so in that sense Zendesk can fulfil the role of a standard ticketing system. However, it is also an omnichannel platform that allows communication across different channels, automates business processes, and even provides answers using an AI. It can be the central inbound communication system for a company, and you can tailor it to many use cases and workflows.

In this book we cover the email, web widget, and website support form parts of that omnichannel platform. Apart from that, Zendesk can also be set up to support customers via chat, phone, and instant messaging.

Many companies of various sizes and types use the platform. For example, Zendesk is used by Siemens, Mailchimp, Tesco, Vodafone, and Charity: Water (to name a few). It's the market leader in this space. You might even have used Zendesk without knowing it. An interaction you had with the customer service department of a business might have happened using Zendesk without you even realising it. Unless you look for it, you won't notice it.

What is Zendesk used for?

Companies typically use Zendesk for inbound support communication. When a customer has a question or an issue and seeks help, they approach the company via their website or app and look for support or contact options.

Most companies offer several different ways for customers to ask for and receive support, and this is where Zendesk can help with their omnichannel capabilities. It ranges from self-service to online forms and email or chats to phone and messaging.

First, the business decides what channels customers can use to request support. Then, they funnel all incoming communication into Zendesk where questions and issues become tickets and customer service Agents help those customers via those tickets. That's where the conversations happen.

Zendesk is very versatile, and it's used in many industries and for many different use cases[10] that include Retail, Software, eCommerce, Healthcare, Facility Management, and internal support such as IT and HR. The use cases seem limitless.

---

[10] See glossary on page 242

What you'll need

This book is a great way to get to know Zendesk from the Customer Service agent's perspective. You won't need anything other than this book to get started, but then all your knowledge will be theoretical. If you put theory to practice, your brain will retain more of this information. Doing practical exercises will help you to absorb what you learn much better.

That's why I included the following exercises in this book. You can follow my instructions step-by-step and experience everything firsthand. I recommend that you practice with Zendesk and see it for yourself. And for this, you will need your own Zendesk account.

It's okay if you don't have access to a paid version of Zendesk. You can sign up for a free trial, which I will show you how to do. It's a try-before-you-buy account with all the essential features. No credit card or payment details are needed. By default, it's valid for 14 days and that should be more than enough to cover everything in this book.

Follow along — Get a free Zendesk account (5 to 10 minutes)

You need the following if you want to complete all the exercises in this book:

- ❏ A computer with internet access
- ❏ A web browser
- ❏ An email address

Sign up for a free Zendesk trial

Open your browser and do the following:

1) **Go to** this Zendesk website: www.zendesk.com/register
2) **Enter the requested details** in the empty web form; most of them are self-explanatory. Feel free to leave out personal information such as your phone number.
3) There are **three items** you need to pay attention to:
   a) Email address
   b) Zendesk name
   c) Password

Last step

Company name | Number of employees

| Berry Ltd ✓ | 100-249 ⌄ |

Your Zendesk subdomain

| berry-peripherals ✓ .zendesk.com |

Choose a name for your Zendesk subdomain. Most people use their team or company name.

Select a language for your Zendesk subdomain:

| English ⌄ |

Create a password

| ········ ✓ 👁 |

Complete trial signup 🖐

By clicking "Complete trial signup" you agree to the Zendesk Master Subscription Agreement and Privacy Policy.

©Zendesk 2021 Privacy Policy Terms & Conditions

Screenshot: Zendesk trial signup form.

The email address

The email address you use needs to be valid. You can use any email address you like (personal or business), but you will need to be able to access it because Zendesk will send you a confirmation message. After you complete the sign-up, you will receive an email with a link to confirm your registration.

Name of your Zendesk account

The form then asks you to fill in "your Zendesk subdomain". This will be the name and web address of your Zendesk. Since Zendesk is cloud-based, you will access it via a web browser[11].

Whatever you enter here becomes the address you will use to access your Zendesk trial account. The system adds ".zendesk.com" to it to turn it into a unique URL. If you enter your company name (e.g. *Berry*), your Zendesk address will be **berry**.zendesk.com.

If the name you entered is already taken, the form will say so and ask you to choose another name. Don't sweat it; find something that isn't already taken and a name that you can easily remember.

---

[11] See *Zendesk Support system requirements* on page 247

The password

The last step is to enter a password. You will need it for logging into your account as an Administrator. Remember the password you enter here.

Complete sign-up and log in

1) After you have entered all the details, you can **complete your sign-up**.

2) Shortly after that, you will **receive an email with a confirmation**. This message confirms your trial sign-up.

3) Now you need to verify and activate your Zendesk trial. **Click on the verification link** and wait for the browser window to show you a confirmation.

That's all you need to activate your account. You can always return to your Zendesk trial by entering your address in the browser's address bar. Notice that you won't need "www" at the beginning—just type yourname.zendesk.com. **yourname** is the name you chose during the sign-up. In our example, it would be **berry**.zendesk.com.

🌐 https://berry.zendesk.com/

Screenshot: Address bar; in our example, the address looks like this.

Tip: Bookmark your Zendesk address in your browser. You will need it for other exercises later. Even if you don't bookmark it, remember your email address and password for later.

Zendesk onboarding and tooltips

When you access your Zendesk trial account, you'll see onboarding instructions for new users. It's a mini-tour through the system that shows you tooltips or asks you to follow specific steps. It helps to familiarise you with the essential elements and some basic functions.

Take a tour

Skip tour and go to setup →

Go
ahead, feel free to go through the instructions and have a look around. It will give you a quick overview. However, the tour may overwhelm you in the beginning because it takes you to the configuration of Zendesk and other sections that are not relevant or are covered later in this book.

That's why **I recommend skipping it for now**. Zendesk gives you the option to do so during one of the onboarding steps. Look for a skip button and press it. We will cover everything you need as an Agent in this book anyway.

Follow along — Activate ticket fields in your trial (5 minutes)

This exercise assumes that you created your trial account as described in the first exercise. You need to activate ticket fields in your trial account because you will need them for our other activities.

We will discuss what ticket fields are and how to use them later. For now, you just need to make the fields available in your trial account.

1) **Click the gear icon** in the navigation bar on the left.
2) Locate the **Manage** section on the left and click on **Ticket Forms**.
3) You should now see the **Default Ticket Form** in the main window.
4) **Click** on it.
5) On the right-hand side, you'll see a box called **Available ticket fields**.
   a) Find **Priority** and **Type** in the list.
   b) Click + or **drag** them to the main window to add them.
   c) They should **show up in the middle section** once you add them. If they are already in the middle section, there is **nothing else to do**.
6) Click **Save** at the bottom right.
7) **Refresh the browser**. In most browsers you can refresh the page as follows:

a) **Ctrl + R** at the same time (on Windows).

b) **Command + R** (on Mac).

c) This makes sure that Zendesk reloads with the ticket fields.

Screenshot: The Default Ticket Form with two active ticket fields.

Foundation

Chapters in this section:

- What is a ticket?
- Where do tickets come from?
- Who creates tickets?
- What's your role in Zendesk?
- How to navigate Zendesk
- How to log in as an Agent

What is a ticket?

People reach out to a company when they have questions about their products or services by sending their questions and issues via various channels. It's then the job of the company's Customer Service (CS) team to take care of those inquiries.

The communication between a customer and a company takes place in an object called a ticket. Tickets contain the conversation between the customer and Customer Support, no matter if they came in via email, chat or phone. Tickets have a unique reference number that we refer to as the **Ticket ID** or **Ticket Number**.

Storing the communication in tickets makes many things simpler: the conversation is in one place, in chronological order, and often with a beginning, middle, and end. The business records what the CS team communicates to the customers. The Ticket Number also allows us to refer to these conversations and enables the company to measure and review them. Managers can check the performance and discover trends within the customer queries.

Tickets contain a lot of information:

- The customer's contact details
- A question or the description of an issue

- When it was received
- The Ticket Number
- Other information depending on the types of ticket data your team needs to gather

Origin of the word "ticket"

When you research the word ticket, you can track it all the way back to the 16th century. It is often associated with a "short written note[12]".

Later, operators used it in places where they would ask a person to fill out a small card for the issue they have. They would fill in contact details and a summary. Operators would then place those cards in a queue of pending queries. Sometimes directly next to an engineer who would deal with the request. The priority would depend on the order of those tickets.

Another variant is the places where you get a ticket upon entering. It's usually a flimsy piece of paper with a number on it that determines your place in the queue. Then you wait as a display or loudspeaker announces the next number in line.

I've been to a government agency recently where that system is still in use. I got a printed ticket and waited for my turn. Old technology, but still works.

---

[12] See bibliography on page 246

Don't call me a number

No one enjoys queuing or falling in line. Of course, you can pull out your smartphone to distract yourself, and you can even pretend to be productive while waiting there, but queuing is usually not what you want in the first place—even if it's the queue in your favourite cafe.

On top of that, it doesn't feel great if someone gives you a number—or worse—calls you a number (unless it's for privacy reasons). No matter if it's in a government agency as I described—it just doesn't feel great.

Given that, try to avoid words with an unfavourable association when talking to customers. Words like a case, problem, or Ticket Number can invoke negative feelings because they are often associated with queuing and time-wasting. No one wants to be just a number in a system.

Tip: The team or business will probably use words such as reference number, which is slightly better than Ticket Number. Even better would be avoiding these altogether by asking for other means of identification: you can often find a customer's ticket by their name, email address, or phone number.

In written communication, you can often get rid of Ticket Numbers entirely. Zendesk can identify most messages automatically and associate them with an existing ticket using the email address, phone number, or social media account. It depends on the type of ticket and how Zendesk is set up.

Overall, it's good to think about how you communicate with your customers, to think about how they will perceive how you speak to them by avoiding terms with a negative association.

Everything revolves around tickets

Tickets in Zendesk are an essential, an indispensable, part of the support you deliver to your customers. Your support conversations and their outcomes revolve around them. They often contain the entire back and forth with a customer—from raising the issue to resolving it. If the customer had several questions, there might be several tickets.

Tickets contain the contact information, description of the inquiry, and other details. When communicating with customers, it is more personal to refer to tickets as "our last interaction" or "the last time we spoke". Don't reduce your customer interactions to just a Ticket Number.

Where do tickets come from?

You need to understand where tickets come from when working on them, and how they are being created in the first place.

Within Zendesk and the industry, the term channel is used to represent a medium for transmission. It's the way of communication for CS, and includes email, social media, instant messaging, and other forms of communication.

Omnichannel

Zendesk is an <u>omnichannel</u>[13] platform. It offers different inbound channels to communicate with customers. The goal for a business and its CS is to be available where the customer is.

Let's imagine a company called *Berry Peripherals Ltd.*, *Berry* for short. A manufacturer of computer peripherals. They produce input devices like keyboards, scanners and webcams as well as output devices such as printers.

---

[13] See glossary on page 242

Berry

However, their best-sellers are keyboards and computer mice in their signature colours strawberry-red and blueberry-blue. They sell their products through their webshop and show them off on social media channels such as Instagram.

Their customers expect to get help online, which is recommended because it makes it easy for prospects and customers to reach out to Customer Service. When selling via your webshop and Instagram you might want to offer support via chat, web forms, and social media.

If your customers prefer to use a different channel, the business needs to consider covering those as well. There is a range of demographics with varying preferences. Managers need to work with the CS team to gather data on what channels work for their End Users.

Whatever channels the business supports, they should all funnel into the same platform, where the CS team can take care of the customers' inquiries and concerns. Using only one platform like Zendesk increases efficiency and productivity.

Channels in Zendesk

The most basic channel is **email**. Zendesk allows an almost unlimited amount of email addresses, and you can share one or several with your customers. Zendesk turns emails sent to those support addresses into tickets.

The company's website or help centre can also host a **web (contact) form**. Here customers can complete their contact information and details of their issue. When submitted, it's turned into a ticket. When the CS team replies, the response goes out via email.

Zendesk also offers live channels such as **chat** and **phone**. These allow customers to chat via the website or the company's app and call in via a phone number provided by the platform. The system stores the conversation or recording on a ticket.

My favourite channel is the **web widget**. It's a container that pops up on the company's website. It combines several channels into one: the website's visitors can search the help centre, chat with an online Agent or (chatbot), request a callback or create a ticket. Any ticket submitted outside of a live chat or call is treated as an email ticket by Zendesk.

Social media and **instant messaging** are other ways to communicate with customers. This is also—you guessed it—stored in tickets.

Besides the channels used by humans, there are some channels for machines. Systems use them to connect to each other and exchange information. Imagine an online system that sends out an error message if something is wrong (for example, when a server is offline). Zendesk allows systems to connect to the platform via their API[14] (an interface between systems), which means that the error message can become a ticket that Zendesk then routes to a team to take care of it, such as Engineering.

Categories of channels

You can classify the various channels in different ways; however, I like to list them in a way that matters from the CS team's perspective. The following is not a hard and fast definition, nor a complete list of supported channels by Zendesk, but it is a useful overview of how companies can use the platform:

- **Passive or self-service** - always available, provides support without or with very little input from the Customer Service team.
  - ○ FAQ, knowledge base, and help centre with helpful articles.
  - ○ Chatbot providing pre-defined answers or referring to existing help centre articles.
- **Asynchronous** - not happening in real-time (not live), where Customer Support can reply with a short or long delay, such as:
  - ○ Email
  - ○ Web forms (the place where users complete a form, e.g. a website)

---

[14] See glossary on page 242

- Forums (where people can ask public questions)
- Social Media (general content visible to everyone)
- Messaging (direct messages)
- **Realtime** - a live conversation between an Agent and a Customer with almost instant replies, such as:
  - Chat
  - Phone
  - Messaging (direct messages)

Did you notice that **messaging** appears in both the Asynchronous and Realtime categories? This is because you can message someone in real-time or delay it. Channels come with different expectations[15]. If someone reaches out via email, they know a reply can take hours or days. If they pick up the phone, they expect someone to pick it up within a minute.

With messaging—be it social, instant messaging or similar—it's different. You might reach out to a company via WhatsApp and have a reply within minutes or hours. Then you take maybe another 15 minutes to pick up your phone and respond to it. Perhaps you are busy or don't feel like responding and instead react to it the next day. In that case, it's a prolonged conversation that's not happening in real-time anymore. It's more like a back and forth comparable to how we use emails.

---

[15] See bibliography on page 246

On the other hand, someone else might respond almost instantly on the messaging platform. This is close to a real-time conversation, because the back and forth happens in quick succession.

For this reason, I put messaging in both categories because it can be both. The company can aim to answer it almost instantaneously like a live chat, but that back and forth via messaging can span hours and days.

Takeaways

Modern companies striving for a good customer experience usually offer omnichannel support. The challenge is which channel to cover and to meet the different Customer expectations.

Follow along — Create a test ticket (5 minutes)

We will have several situations where we'll need a ticket to test or demonstrate something. I will refer to them as **test tickets**. At least one was created for you when you started your Zendesk trial, but you'll need more tickets for upcoming exercises. There are two quick ways to create a new ticket:

→ Add a ticket manually within Zendesk.

→ Send an email that becomes a ticket.

To do that, let's imagine we bought some products from *Berry* (a colourful keyboard and a wireless mouse), but we have some issues with the devices, so we'll reach out to their customer service.

Add a ticket manually within Zendesk

1) Move your cursor over **+Add** (towards the top left corner).

2) Select **New Ticket** and a new tab with a blank ticket will appear.

3) Enter a **subject** (in the middle section of the screen):

A button on my new keyboard came off

4) Add a **comment** in **Public reply** (beneath the subject):

Hello Support,

The space bar on my keyboard came off. How can I fix this?

5) Set the **Requester** (on the left) by entering a name or email. You can enter any email address here or use the default customer in your trial: type in **The Customer** or enter his email **customer@example.com**.

6) Click on **Submit** (lower right corner).

Don't worry about the meaning of ticket comments and Requester for now. We will go over all elements in the following chapters. Close all tabs in Zendesk.

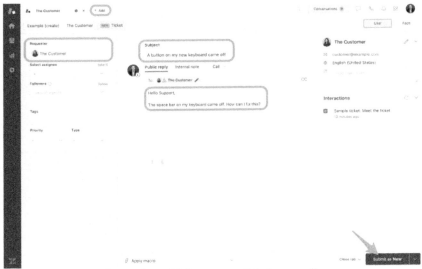

Screenshot: Adding a new ticket manually.

Create a ticket via an email

1) Open your personal email inbox and **create a new email**.

2) Enter the following **email address** in the "To"-field:

support@**yourname**.zendesk.com.

In our example from earlier, it would be support@berry.zendesk.com.

3) Enter a **subject**:

Mouse not connecting

4) Then **add some text** in the email body:

Hello support,
My wireless mouse is not connecting to my computer anymore.
Please help.

5) Click **Send**.

You might wonder how I know the email address of your Zendesk? The answer is simple: Zendesk creates at least one email address by default for every account. Your trial account will be available via support@**yourname**.zendesk.com. That's great for testing the system.

Find your test tickets

Within a minute or two, you should see a new ticket in your Views, which is the place where you can find all tickets in your Zendesk. Each View is a list of specific types of tickets. For example, **All unsolved tickets** shows all tickets that don't have a final resolution. We will cover Views in more detail in a later chapter.

For now, check for your new tickets.

1) Go to **Views** (click on the inbox folder in the panel on the very left).

2) Select **All unsolved tickets** from the list.

3) You should then see a **list of tickets** in the central part of the window, including those you just created.

Screenshot: Go to Views > All unsolved tickets to see your test tickets.

These are our **test tickets**. You'll need them in the other exercises. When asked to create more test tickets, you can always return to this section and follow the steps above to generate more.

Who creates tickets?

We need to look at the people that create the tickets in Zendesk. You already know how Zendesk creates tickets. It's equally important to understand who created them.

There are certain terminologies within the industry, and some are specific to Zendesk. We'll have a look at these in more detail:

- Customer
- End User
- Requester

We will use *Berry* as an example: their products are enjoyed by consumers for their vivid colours and by professionals for their high quality and durability.

Customer

So far, I've used the term Customer to describe anyone that reaches out to your team. It is an excellent term to describe buyers or consumers of your products or services. Zendesk uses this word to describe a wide range of people, and I will use it similarly.

It's a pretty standard term. People outside the industry should understand what or who you are talking about.

For *Berry*, anyone who bought a product is a Customer—regardless of where they bought it.

During a meeting, you might hear: "We have an influx of new Customers thanks to our outbound marketing activities. Be ready for an uptick in tickets." In other words, business is going well, and more people likely have questions that will cause more tickets.

End User

Sometimes the word Customer does not fit that well. For example, when we talk about users of our software or about internal users. The IT department will probably use the phrase End User rather than Customer or colleague. It helps to distinguish the role they play within the system.

An End User is a more technical term and shared within the industry. Outside a business, however, people might not know the meaning.

Within Zendesk, the term End User and Customer are often used interchangeably. An End User is anyone who reaches out to you via any available channel and creates tickets.

Every Customer that reached out to *Berry's* Customer Service via Zendesk, is an End User in Zendesk. But not all Customers contact CS—so not all Customers are End Users.

In a conversation, you might hear someone from IT say: "There are currently 12,500 End Users in Zendesk and we have 84,000 registered Customers in our online shop." That means that you have more people shopping via the website

(84,000 Customers) than people that reached out to support (12,500 End Users). That's ok, considering that you don't want every Customer to open a ticket.

Requester

Customers represent virtually everyone your company does business with. End Users are a subset of people within Zendesk. And Requester is an even more specific term. This is the person on a ticket that requested help. Anytime a Customer creates a ticket, they become a new End User in Zendesk (unless they already have an End User account).

The Requester is a very technical term and is used in help desk and ticketing systems. People within the Customer Support industry should understand this term.

If someone contacted *Berry's* team via email, website support form, or chat, you would find an email address (and often a name). Tickets from phone calls would have a phone number instead of the name of the Requester.

You might hear colleagues say: "Who's the requester on that ticket?" or "Search Zendesk for the email of that End User. I want to see if he requested any more tickets."

And what can they do within Zendesk?

Customers can usually only submit tickets via the active support channels. If Zendesk Guide is activated and configured to allow End Users to log in, they can review and update tickets, but what they can see and do is limited.

So what's an End User again?

If we were to put these terms in a hierarchy, it would look like this:

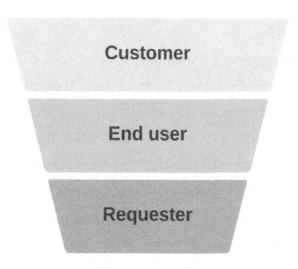

- **Customer** - a general term that describes all people buying or consuming your products or services.
- **End User** - an industry term meaning everyone whose contact details are within Zendesk. Only Customers submitting a ticket become an End User.
- **Requester** - a technical term within Zendesk and the industry that signifies a user who has requested help via a ticket.

Unfortunately, these terms are sometimes used interchangeably within Zendesk and their user guides, which can make it hard to differentiate them at first.

What's your role in Zendesk?

Let's have a closer look at the other side: who works inside Zendesk? If someone creates tickets, then there must be people that work on them. Zendesk refers to these people as Agents.

Agents are also often called Customer Service representatives, the Customer happiness team, or sometimes the "support guys". There is a range of job titles out there describing the same thing. In a nutshell, whenever a Customer sends in a question or inquires about something, it's an Agent's job to help them.

In this book, we focus on the perspective of the Agent and how to help Customers. However, we'll also cover the all support staff roles that have access to Zendesk:

- Agent
- Administrator
- Account Owner

Berry Ltd is a growing organisation with people filling various roles. Their Zendesk has Agents, Admins and an Account Owner.

Agent

Zendesk describes the people that work on tickets as Agents. Since you are reading this book, this is probably your role.

Agents represent the company when communicating with End Users and it's their responsibility to provide support, to help the Requestor find the answers they need, and that is done via tickets.

Agent is a specific term within Zendesk, but it's also widely used within the industry, and you will see it used in job titles and descriptions.

Within Zendesk, Agents have a defined range of things that they are authorised to do. This typically includes but is not limited to:

- Access and update tickets
- Access and edit End User details
- Create and edit their own Macros and Views
- View reports

This is not a complete list, but gives you an idea of what they can do. These privileges can be limited (or increased) by Administrators.

Assignee

On a ticket, you'll find the Assignee field. In most cases, this is the Agent that works on or solves the ticket. The Assignee is a term also used by other ticketing systems.

Let's imagine *Tom*, a Customer Service Agent for *Berry*. In a conversation, he might say: "I'm working on the ticket, I'm the Assignee," or "Can you assign the ticket to me, please. I will reply to the Customer later."

Groups

In Zendesk, Agents (and other support roles) are organised into Groups. The people within a Group belong to the same organisational unit. Groups can reflect company departments such as Customer Service, Accounting, IT support, etc. Groups can also reflect a function or skill, such as *Technical Support* or *English Support*

Agents need to be in at least one Group, but can belong to more than one. *Tom* is part of the support team and speaks English. In *Berry's* Zendesk he is a member of two Groups: *Level 1 Support* and *English Support*. If *Tom* spoke Spanish as well, his managers would also include him in the *Spanish Support* Group.

Tickets can be assigned to individual Agents or a Group. How is that useful? When a Spanish-speaking End User submits a ticket, it can be routed to the *Spanish Support* Group. If *Tom* belongs to that Group, he can work on the ticket and help the Customer.

Admins can also control the visibility of tickets by using Groups. In our example, they might make the View for *Spanish Support* visible only to members of that Group. This means anyone that doesn't speak Spanish (and is not part of that Group) will not be able to see those tickets and therefore they won't be distracted by tickets that they can't work on.

Group is a relatively generic term in the industry, but within Zendesk it has a specific meaning and use.

During meetings, people might say: "All technical tickets should be directly assigned to Level 2 (Group)." or "Tom, can you assign the ticket back to the group so that the others can pick it up."

Administrator

There is another role within Zendesk called Administrator, or Admin for short. They usually work "behind the scenes" setting up channels, business rules, and designing and implementing workflows. While Agents spend most of their time interacting with End Users, Admins typically focus on the system's configuration.

Admin(istrator) is a widely used term across the IT landscape and is not specific to Zendesk. You might find it in job descriptions and titles.

Admin privileges include everything an Agent can do, but on top of that they can also:

- Create Groups and Organisations (more on that later)
- Add and manage End Users, Agents, and Admins
- Edit and view reports
- Access, create, and edit business rules
- Access and control settings of the entire platform
- Install and configure apps

This is not an exhaustive list, but it's an overview of the main capabilities compared to Agents.

Admins are Agents too

Let me repeat this important point: **Administrators have the same rights as Agents**. Admins can perform all the actions an Agent can within Zendesk.

Let's take *Robert* as an example, he works in IT at *Berry Ltd*. He knows Zendesk very well and management made him an Administrator. He can be an Assignee on a ticket, the team can assign tickets to the *IT* Group or directly to *Robert*. He can then work on and solve the ticket—the same way an Agent can.

Also, like Agents, Admins can belong to Groups. A Group can contain both Agents and Admins. In some companies, Admins work alongside Agents to solve tickets and they only use their extra privileges to make changes in the system when needed.

Within Zendesk, both roles are sometimes lumped together. For example, if a manager asks "What's the number of Agents in our Zendesk?" or when a setting allows visibility for "all

Agents", both Agents and Admins are included. However, when referring to people who have access to Zendesk settings, these are Admins.

In conversations, you will hear things like "The Admin needs to update the Macros for the Level 2 Support." or "the Admin needs to create a new View for the Group."

Account Owner

The last role you need to know about is the Account Owner. They are technically the same as Administrators, they can do the same things, but they can also manage account licensing and payment details:

- Subscription details
- Billing and payment
- Account changes

There can be only one Account Owner in a Zendesk account. This user handles the subscription, billing, and payment management details. The Account Owner can also promote other Admins in Zendesk to become a billing Admin so that they can manage subscription and billing details as well.

Robert from IT might say to the CS manager "We need to add two more Agents for your team, but we are out of licenses. Let's ask William, the COO. He can add them—he's the Account Owner." Similarly, in a management meeting someone might ask "Who manages the payment details of our Zendesk account?" and the answer would be *William*, the Account Owner (or a billing Admin he appointed).

So what's an Agent again?

If we were to put these terms in a hierarchy, it would look like this:

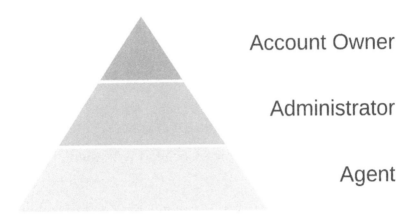

- **Account Owner** - Technically an Admin with extra privileges. A unique user with the most admin privileges.
- **Admin** - the Administrators of the system. They can work on tickets as well but usually focus on configuring the system.
- **Agent** - the Customer Service Representative. Their job is to help Customers. They work on and solve tickets.

The Account Owner can do what the Admins can do. Administrators have the same rights as Agents, but they can't access the things the Account Owner can. Agents can work on tickets, but they cannot access the settings the Admins and Account Owner have access to.

Tip: When I refer to Agents in this book, it includes Admins and Account Owners. They have the same user rights as Agents, and it keeps things simpler. If there is something only a specific role can do, e.g. an Admin, I will mention that.

You will notice Zendesk does the same in the user interface and in their documentation. Admins and Account Owners are lumped together.

Who determines the role of a user?

Every user must have a role associated with them: End User, Agent or Admin.

End Users are automatically created by Zendesk when the user submits his first ticket. Agents and Admins have to be manually set up by another Administrator or the Account Owner.

How to navigate Zendesk

Every Agent and Admin needs to move between different parts of Zendesk. Therefore, you need to know how to access the main areas of the system.

Here are the main sections of Zendesk interface:

- Navigation bar
- Top bar
- Main window

You can access the various pages via the navigation and top bar: open the page you want to see by clicking the related icon.

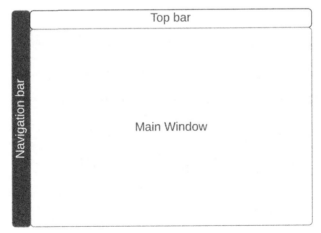

Figure: Navigation bar on the left, top bar, and main window.

Navigation bar

The navigation bar is always on the left side, is almost always visible, and contains the icons you use to navigate to the different parts of Zendesk. The colour of the navigation bar can be changed by an Admin. The icons you see depend on how your Zendesk is set up, but you should always at least see the following (from top to bottom):

- **Home icon**. This leads to the home page or dashboard. This is your start page by default after you log in. In a trial version, it shows a **Getting Started** page with instructions and tips. In a paid account, it leads to the **Dashboard**, which shows a range of information such as updates to your tickets, tickets assigned to you and your Groups, as well as some ticket statistics.

- **Views icon**. This icon displays the Views page, which contains the list of Views of your tickets. They are one of the fastest ways to see and access tickets. We go over that in much more detail in a later chapter.

- **Admin icon**. The Admin icon displays the Admin Home page, which you use to access the settings available to your user role.

You might see other icons in your navigation bar. It depends on the version and configuration of your Zendesk. Additional icons can appear before or after the Admin icon. But the main ones (Home, Views, and Admin) should always be available.

Top bar

The top bar is always at the top of the interface, and is almost always visible. Here you will see open tabs (for tickets) and have access to a few other parts of Zendesk. The available icons can differ, but you should at least see the following (left to right):

- **+Add** (left side, to the right of the last open tab) is a multi-select button: click on it to create a new ticket. Hover over it, and it allows you to add a new User, Organisation, Ticket, or Search (depending on your user privileges). Below that, it shows recently viewed tickets. Clicking one of the options opens a window or tab to enter more details.

- **Search** (a magnifying glass icon on the right side of the bar). Access the search via this icon. Enter words or a Ticket Number and press enter. Zendesk will show you users, tickets, and other results related to the search term. More on that in another chapter.

- **Products** (somewhere right of the magnifying glass). Click on this to open (or switch between) other Zendesk products. The products you see and have access to depends on your role.

- **Profile** (top right corner). Allows you to look at your user profile and a range of other information. Have a look at your user profile to see details such as role and profile picture. More information on that later.

- **Tabs** (one or more). When you open a ticket or run a search, you will see how the top bar fills up with different tabs. Tabs allow you to jump between tickets, profiles, and search results quickly. It can come in handy if you are working on several things at the same time. Ticket tabs typically disappear when you are done with them. If they stay open and you don't need them any longer, you can close them manually.

In addition to those standard icons and tabs, there might be other icons visible in the top bar. This depends on the version and configuration of your Zendesk. The main ones (Add, Search, and Profile) should always be available.

Main window

The main window shows content depending on what you select in the navigation or top bar. Zendesk can display Views, settings, tickets—whatever is relevant to the task at hand.

Tip: You can access a lot of the pages in Zendesk via a direct link. Bookmark them in your browser for direct access later. Go to the Views (click on the Views icon in the navigation bar on the left) and have a look at the address bar of your browser. You should see something like this https://berry.zendesk.com/Agent/filters/...

In your account, you probably see

https://**yourname**.zendesk.com/Agent/filters/**1234567890**

→ **yourname** is the name of your Zendesk

→ **1234567890** is the internal name/number in Zendesk for a specific View

Now try to enter

https://yourname.zendesk.com/Agent/filters/

- Replace **yourname** with your account name
- Remove the number at the end

You will see the Views page with the first View in the list selected. You can Bookmark this link to quickly access the list of Views (or a specific View if you don't remove the number).

This can come in handy when you are logging in and want to bypass the start page. Keep an eye out for URLs; a lot of other parts of Zendesk can be directly accessed like this.

How to log in as an Agent

When you sign up for a trial account, you become the Account Owner with Admin rights. This means you can access all the settings and features an Agent typically would not be exposed to.

For our exercises, however, I will need you to log in as an Agent. Therefore, you need to create another user account with Agent privileges. This way, you can experience the point of view from that role. I'll show you how to accomplish this within Zendesk.

Follow along — Set up your Agent (5 to 10 minutes)

This assumes you created your trial account as previously described and that you have added the ticket fields as instructed in Follow along — Activate ticket fields in your trial.

You need the following to continue:

❏ Your existing Zendesk trial account login. That's the email address and password you used to create your trial. Let's call it **Admin user** and **email A**.

❏ Another email address for your Agent account, let's refer to it as **Agent user** and **email B**.

Your **email A** is associated with your **Admin user**. If you log in using that email and associated password, you have all the rights of an Admin. To experience the perspective of an Agent, you will need a separate user. That can only be achieved by creating a new **Agent user**—and therefore, you need a different email address.

Use a separate email address for the **Agent user**. I'm sure you have several personal or professional emails at your disposal. If not, you can create a new one. There are many free email providers out there, without endorsing one in particular; here are some options (in alphabetical order): Gmail, Outlook, Yahoo[16].

This step is necessary if you want to see the Agent experience and follow along with future exercises.

Add a new user

1) Go to the **navbar** of your Zendesk trial.

2) Move your cursor over **+Add**.

3) Select **User**.

4) On the new page, **enter the following**:

5) **Name the user.**

    a) Enter your **first name** and the word **Agent**. My first name is Nils; in my test accounts, you would often find **Nils Agent** as a user. It's not very imaginative, but it gets the job done. Also,

---

[16] See bibliography on page 246

it allows you to differentiate your **Admin** from your **Agent user**.

   b) Alternatively, just call the new Agent user *Tom*.

6) Enter the email for that user (again, this needs to be different from your **Admin user**).

7) Select **Staff Member** under user type.

8) Next, choose **Agent** as a role. In case you don't see the Agent role as an option, select **Staff** from the list.

9) Click **Add**.

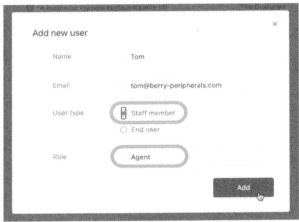

Screenshot: Add new user

Zendesk then takes you to the user profile of that Agent. You don't need to do anything here. Close the tab, and your job here is done.

Log in as the Agent

To log in as an Agent, you first need to sign out as the Administrator. That ensures you don't mix up the users.

1) Go to the **navbar**.
2) Click on your **user profile** in the top right.
3) Select **Sign out**.

Now log in as an Agent. Check your inbox of **email B** and look for the welcome message from Zendesk.

Did you forget the password for that **Agent user**? No, Zendesk does not ask you for a password. Instead, the system sends a link in that email that allows you to set up a personal password.

Check to verify that you received the email. If yes, follow the instructions to set a password and sign in. Check your spam folder if you don't see the welcome email from Zendesk.

If you didn't receive the email with instructions, do the following:

1) Go to your Zendesk trial **login page**.
2) Click **Forgot my password.**
3) Enter the email of the **Agent user**.
4) Click **Submit**.
5) Look for the **welcome email**.

6) **Click the link** in that email and create a new password on the website.

After you've set the password, you should automatically sign in. If not, go to your Zendesk trial login page page and enter **email B** with your new password.

Why does it matter?

On the surface, you won't see much difference when you're signed in as an Agent. However, if you click to access the Admin settings (gear icon in the navigation bar), you will see considerably fewer options there. That's ok, that's what we want.

From now on, unless mentioned otherwise, please follow along with any instructions logged in as the **Agent user**. This is the best way to experience the point of view from the role of an Agent.

Working With Tickets

Chapters in this section:

- Diving into ticket comments
- Zooming in on ticket fields
- Applying a Status to tickets
- Updating tickets with Macros
- Reviewing the Customer
- Moving between tickets

Diving into ticket comments

Customers are going to send in their questions, and we are going to reply to them. Here, simple communication skills, such as reading and writing, are required. If they contact us by phone, then it's all about listening and talking. Of course, I know it's basic, but please bear with me.

There is also the aspect of how to deliver excellent Customer Service. That includes people skills, sometimes referred to as soft skills. Experts have written extensively on the topic, and they are far more qualified than I am in that aspect, so we'll focus mainly on the actions you need to take in Zendesk to get the Customers' answers.

Zendesk uses comments to capture the written conversation on a ticket. For example, the Requester sends an email, Zendesk then converts the email's content into the first comment of a new ticket. If you open the ticket tab, you will read the Customer's query and—if you can assist—reply. Updating the ticket with a comment updates the ticket.

As a result, every ticket has comments, typically the first comment of an End User and the Agent's reply. A ticket can contain many comments; it's usual to have several questions and answers on a single ticket. This back and forth between the Requester and support team makes up the conversation on a ticket.

If you read carefully and try to understand the Requester's issue, you might be able to help them immediately. The best possible outcome is solving a ticket with just one answer. In the industry, this is referred to as a "one-touch ticket". And it's a standard metric in the CS space. It can tell a manager how thorough a person is.

Get a closer look at ticket comments

A ticket will open in a new tab when you click on it. It will take up the whole main window in Zendesk. You will see a lot of elements on the page. Let's ignore the side panels on the left and right and focus on the ticket comments in the middle section.

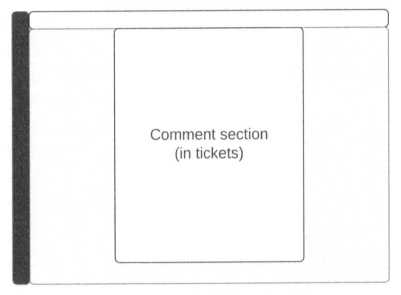

Figure: Comment section in the main window.

Depending on your version of Zendesk and whether the ticket is a new or an existing ticket, what you see might differ. The comment box might be in the upper part or at the lower end of your ticket page. However, the functionality remains the same.

The two types of ticket comments

In Zendesk, you will find two kinds of comments: public and internal. On a ticket, Zendesk refers to them as a **Public reply** and an **Internal note**.

- **Public reply** is a comment that can be read by any user who has access to the ticket in Zendesk. This includes both the Requester plus anyone that is CC'd on the ticket. Every public comment added to a ticket sends a notification to the Requester (and everyone added as a CC). If it's an email ticket, the Requester will receive an email with your public comment. The Requester can reply to that email, and that reply will be captured as another public comment on the same ticket. That is the cyclic back-and-forth of a conversation, as described earlier.

- **Internal notes** are private comments that are only visible to Agents. They are not visible to the Requester or other CC'd End Users. Only CC'd Agents or those added as Followers will receive a notification when an internal note is added. A yellow background highlights internal notes on tickets. You can have tickets with only private comments; they are referred to as private tickets.

On the ticket, you can switch between public and private comments. Select either **Public reply** or **Internal note**. When you switch to the internal note, you will notice how the comment box changes to a yellow background. A public reply is displayed as black text on a white background.

Tip: Whenever you want to note something down for yourself or share details with others, use private comments. Zendesk stores them within the ticket, and anyone with access rights can read them later. This can be useful if you want to remember something for the next time you look at the ticket or share information and instructions with other Agents.

In a conversation, someone might say "Can you please reply to the Customer on ticket 12345?" This would imply that you send a public comment since End Users can only see public replies. Alternatively, someone in your company might tell you "Put the details in an internal note and assign the ticket to the team lead," which means you've been asked to summarise what you know and assign the ticket to someone else.

Adding CC and changing the To-field

You will notice some familiar functionalities from email messages: the **CC** and **To** fields. They work pretty similarly, too.

- **CC** (or Carbon Copy) is used to add other users to a ticket. You can CC one or several users; simply enter an email address to add an existing user or a new one. The recipients will receive public comments via notifications. This way, everyone who is CC'd can respond and add a public reply, which of course, is seen by everyone on the ticket (Assignee, Requester, CC'd users). You can always remove CC'd users, but you must do that before making a ticket update that you don't want them to see.

- **To** is the email address of the ticket Requester, but you can also use this field to change the Requester. There can be only one Requester in the To- field. Enter the name or email of an existing user, or add a new email address (which creates a new user) in Zendesk. They receive public comments by default and can reply to them.

The To- field is crucial because this user is the ticket Requester, the person that needs assistance with something. So don't change it unless you want to change the ticket Requester.

Keep an eye on the CC field as well because End Users can add someone as a CC when sending a ticket via email, which means that they are added to the CC field of a ticket. As a result, they will receive every public comment added to the ticket.

Text formatting and attachments

Like with any other proper text editor, you can also format the text in your comments. Formatting is activated by default and allows some standard rich text options, including highlighting text as **bold** or *italic*, adding hyperlinks, and more.

If activated, you can also add attachments. There is an option to add one or several files from your computer. Likewise, you can drag and drop them onto the ticket. If you drag a file onto the ticket, you have the option to add it in line with the text or as an attachment. The first option is helpful if you want to place images such as screenshots at a specific place in your comment to help explain something. The second option is more beneficial for adding standalone text and data files.

Other elements, such as the Emoji-Selector, may appear. These additional features are situational and depend on the ticket channel.

Tip: Generally speaking, the lower you keep the number of back and forths between yourself and the Customer, the better. The Customer experience improves if minimal effort is required on their part. You might remember a situation you experienced when you felt that the other party didn't understand what you said or wrote, and their response seemed as if they didn't read your message. Instead of getting a helpful answer, you were left with another question. This can be frustrating. Fewer, more thorough replies are better than many quick ones — always focus on quality over quantity.

Summary

A ticket conversation is contained within its comments. Therefore, as in any conversation, it's necessary to be careful about what you say. The Agent is in control of the visibility of comments. The internal comments may also help to document or pass on information to another Agent. Other than that, text formatting, attaching images and files, and adding CCs are similar to the email experience.

Zooming in on ticket fields

Everyone working with tickets in Zendesk will come across ticket fields. These are properties where specific information is stored within the ticket. When a user submits a ticket, Zendesk adds a lot of details. Other details are added by users.

Email tickets are a good example. The ticket's subject is taken from the email subject, and the comment comes from the email body. When an End User submits a ticket via the help centre or a website form, they fill in some details. Those details are stored in the ticket and some of this information translates directly to ticket fields.

There are two kinds of ticket fields

- **System fields** are the default fields that come out-of-the-box with Zendesk. Some can be slightly modified or added. But for the most part, the options are limited. Companies often want to gather more information that's not covered by system fields. In those cases, Admins will add custom fields.

- **Custom fields** can be set up to store additional details not covered by the system fields. They offer the customisability a company often needs to tailor their workflows.

You will come across different ticket fields, no matter if they are system or custom fields. Here are the most frequently used ones in Zendesk accounts, based on my observation and years of experience.

Most common or useful field types

- **Drop-down list** offers a predefined selection of options. The End User or Agent can pick one when they create the ticket. Admins can set a default selection, but that's optional. They are by far the most common and helpful way of storing details in a ticket. Typical uses cases are the categorisation of elements, as in the following examples:
    - ○ Type of inquiry: price inquiry, order update, product support
    - ○ Product category: Keyboards, Scanners, Webcams
    - ○ Specific product: Webcam HD, Webcam Pro 700, Webcam Pro 800
- **Checkbox**, sometimes referred to as tick-box, allows users to choose a yes/no or on/off answer. They are helpful if you want to capture just one of two choices instead of a long list of options. Here are some examples of how a checkbox can be used:

- o   Ask if a user wants to be added to a newsletter
- o   Flag an End User as a premium Customer in Zendesk
- **Decimal field** contains numeric input with decimals. They are often used to store the value of products or services. Some examples:
  - o   Order value (in $)
  - o   Refund (in €)
  - o   Shoe size

Close up on system fields

We already know four system fields; we covered them in the chapter about ticket comments:

- To
- CC
- Subject
- Description

You can find those fields in the comment section (or middle part) of the ticket. All the other ticket fields are on the left-hand side of a ticket (in the ticket panel).

Let's zoom in on the ticket fields. When you open up a new or existing ticket, you'll find them between the navigation bar and the comment section. It's important to understand what they mean, so we will cover them from top to bottom:

- Requester
- Assignee
- Follower
- Tags
- Type
- Priority
- Custom

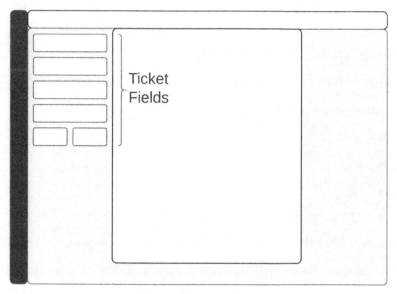

Figure: Ticket field panel on the left.

Requester

This is usually the person who sent this request in the first place. In that case, it's set automatically. But an Agent can create a new ticket for or in the name of someone–that user will be the Requester on that ticket. Creating a ticket this way is practical when the Requester is not submitting a query via the usual channels.

Either way, every ticket requires one Requester (and one only). You can change the Requester on a ticket, but if the Requester is removed, that person will no longer receive updates of that ticket. If, for some reason, you need to change the Requester, consider adding the user as a Follower or CC to keep them informed.

Assignee

This is the person or Group that is responsible for the ticket. A ticket can be assigned to an Agent or a Group. But a ticket can only have one Assignee. In this context, a Group counts as one Assignee. If you need to add more people, you can add them as a Follower or CC. Click on this field to see all available Assignees.

Tip: If you can help the Requester with a ticket, it's common to assign it to yourself. This shows the ownership of the ticket and also means you are responsible for it. By default, Zendesk will assign it to you only when you solve a ticket. But there is the **Take it** option next to the Assignee field. When you click it, the ticket is assigned to you.

In case you can't help the Customer, you want to assign the ticket to someone else. If it's a small team, you might know exactly who to choose. In mid-sized and larger teams, however, you want to assign it to a Group.

For example, you work in tech support and a Customer has a question about his order. Only the people in the orders team have access to the shopping system. So you assign it to that Group.

By the way, the trial account has only one Group, so you can't experiment much with this. But in real life, it's a common thing to move around tickets or to escalate them.

Follower

This is a field for Agents and not End Users. You can compare it to BCC as no End User will see the list of Followers on a ticket. Followers will receive notifications on updates.

Tip: Use Followers to place Agents on a ticket to keep them in the loop or for training new Agents on how more tenured colleagues handle specific requests. They will receive public and internal comments and can reply to the ticket.

If you want to move the responsibility of a ticket to someone else, you have to assign the ticket to a Group or Agent and put yourself as a Follower if you want to see what happens to the ticket.

Tags

Tags represent more details that we want to add to a ticket. When added, you can use Tags to find specific tickets later, or managers can use them to use them in reports. You can add them manually by typing into the field. They can also be added by Macros, ticket fields, business rules, or apps. All Tags are saved as lowercase, even if you enter them with capital letters.

Type

In Zendesk, tickets can be one of four Types. Like Tags, you can use the Type field to categorise tickets, find them in the search or use it for reporting. You can leave this field blank, but you can choose one of these options:

- **Question** simply means the Requester has a question that needs to be answered.
- **Incident** can imply a minor issue that needs to be taken care of. However, if several users report the same problem, you can turn those tickets into incidents and link them to a problem. For that to work, a problem ticket needs to exist first. If that's the case, you can select an incident and choose the problem from a drop-down field.
- **Problem** indicates a major issue with a product or service that needs to be resolved. It's typically used to indicate an issue affecting multiple End Users — for example, the outage of a website or a critical

application not running. If incidents are linked to a problem, you can update them all in one go.

- **Task** is something that needs to be acted on later. As soon as you turn a ticket into a task, an extra field with a due date appears. The task is automatically scheduled at 12 pm of the due date you select. You might use Task in a View to keep an eye on all tickets with a due date.

Priority

The Priority field is not required but can be helpful to indicate how urgent something is. In an ideal world, everything is taken care of immediately, but when that's not possible, a company needs to prioritise who to help first.

In that case, it's helpful to pick one of the four options (Low, Normal, High, Urgent). Using this field allows you to sort tickets by Priority, search for them, or use them in reporting. They can be set manually or automatically by the system.

<u>Custom fields</u>

All activated and visible system fields are in the ticket panel on the left. Admins can change settings for some of those system fields (for example, toggle their visibility). Others might appear depending on specific functionality.

Custom ticket fields typically show up below the system fields. They usually contain anything that is not already addressed by the system fields. Custom fields might be used for the ticket category, a list of products, or virtually anything else that needs to be tracked in a ticket. The order of the fields can vary because Admins can change how they are displayed. By default, a Zendesk trial comes with system fields only.

Recap

Apart from comments, tickets can hold much more information. They are stored in system fields and custom fields. Many different field types are available. How the Admins utilise them depends on the workflows that have been set up.

Follow along — Update a comment and a ticket field (5 minutes)

We just covered quite a bit of ground. Let us see it in action and play with comments and ticket fields. This exercise assumes that you are logged as your **Agent user**.

1) Bring up one of your test tickets:

   a) Go to **Views**.

   b) Select **All unsolved tickets** from the list.

   c) **Click on one** of the tickets you created in the previous exercise, e.g. the one with the subject *"Mouse not connecting."*

2) **Add someone as a CC** (optional) to see how it looks from the Agent perspective and as an End User. Note that whoever you add as a CC will receive email notifications when you submit a ticket with a public comment.

3) **Write a comment** to pretend that you are replying to the email you've just sent to yourself. Yes, talk to yourself. Go ahead. No, don't do it out loud. That would be weird. But it's ok to talk to yourself on a ticket:

   Hello dear customer,

   So sorry to hear that you have trouble with your device.

   Please try to turn it off and on again.

   With regards.

Screenshot: Ticket fields and comments.

4) Play around with the **formatting**.

    a) Turn the second line to *italic*.

    b) Make the third row **bold**.

5) Switch to an **internal note** to see how it looks (black text on a yellow background). You can leave it like this, but then the Requester won't get an email.

6) Switch it back to **public reply** (it's now black text on a white background again). With this setting, Zendesk sends out an email to the Requester and everyone that is CC'd.

7) Then move to the ticket fields on the left:

    a) Click on the element for the **Assignee**.

    b) Select the **Support** Group.

8) **Add a Follower**, for example, your Admin user.

9) **Add a Tag** to the ticket. Write one or several words in the Tag field, e.g. **gold_support**. Separate words will

result in separate Tags, but if you use an underline or hyphen between words, it turns into a one-word Tag. You can add several of them without a comma; Zendesk adds all of them as Tags.

10) Select a **Type**.

   a) Select **Task** from the drop-down.

   b) You'll notice how the due date field will pop up underneath. **Pick a date** in the future.

11) Lastly, choose a **Priority**. You are the Requester. This certainly requires the highest Priority: set it to **Urgent**.

12) That should be pretty much everything. We meddled with comments and fields. You can now **click submit** (at the bottom right) to save the ticket.

13) After a moment, Zendesk will have everything processed. You can **check your email** and have a look at the notification.

If you are still on the ticket, stay right there. If the ticket tab is closed, bring up the ticket again.

Tip: Compare what you see as an Agent in Zendesk with what's visible to the End User via email. You should see quite a difference. You can repeat the process with different variables, choosing other options. Experiment with the Requester, CC, and public vs internal comments.

It's ok to talk to yourself. Go ahead and try this with your own email addresses. You can add other people's email addresses, but give them a heads up because your trial account is sending out real emails.

Applying a Status to tickets

Personal and professional emails usually have one of two states: unread or read. When working with tickets, we have more options. In Zendesk and similar systems, it's called a Ticket Status, and we need to give some thought to what Status you want to set on a given ticket.

Unread and read might be enough for personal messages, but a support process requires a more granular way of tracking progress.

That's why Zendesk allows a ticket to have one of several Statuses. It's another system field, but I'm giving it its own spotlight here to talk about its importance in the ticket life cycle.

Here is an overview of the options:

- **New**
- **Open**
- **Pending**
- **On-hold**
- **Solved**
- **Closed**

New

This indicates a new ticket; no action has been taken yet. This Status is set by Zendesk automatically. Once the Status has been changed, it can never be set back to New.

Open

This is a ticket that has been assigned and is no longer New. It indicates that an Agent needs to do something here: reply to a question, for example. You can select the Open Status manually to signal that it needs to be worked on.

Pending

This indicates that the Agent waits for a reply from the Requester. You want to choose this when you reply to a Customer and ask for more details. Zendesk automatically changes a ticket back to the Open Status when a Customer replies to that ticket.

On-hold (optional)

This Status also shows that we are waiting for an action or information, but in this case, it's not from the Requester. It could instead be from another Agent, another department, or a third party outside Zendesk. The ticket is also changed back to Open when someone replies to it. This Status is optional and, by default, not activated in your trial account.

Solved

This is the target state of every ticket. This implies that all questions have been answered and that all queries are taken care of–when we consider it done. You want to put it in this state when no further action is required. Any ticket that's Solved but not Closed can also be reopened if an end-user replies to it.

Closed tickets

Tickets in this Status are effectively archived. You can still find them and access them, but no further changes or updates are possible. An Agent can't select this Status; it's applied automatically by the system after a given time. The default delay is four days but can be adjusted by an Admin.

Submit tickets with a Status

Every ticket has a **Submit** button (on the bottom right) where you can select one of the Statuses available. For you as an Agent, this is **Open, Pending, Solved**, and **On-hold** (optional).

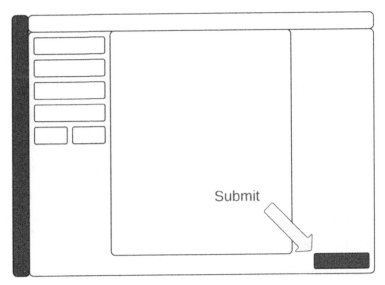

Figure: Submit button on a ticket.

The submit button actually has two functions: apply a chosen Status and save the ticket. When you click the submit button, any updates or changes, any comment you made on a ticket will be saved, including the Status you choose. The business rules will then process everything in the background, which might include sending out notifications or assigning tickets.

Tip: Or rather a heads up–the ticket will be saved (and messages sent out) only if you click Submit (with any Status). I don't mean to repeat myself, but I wanted to emphasise this fact.

When I work with Customer Service teams, it's not always clear what the Submit button does, especially if they are not familiar with Zendesk or cloud-based tools in general.

This meant that people thought that they had replied to a Customer when all they had done was enter a comment, change some ticket fields, and then close the tab. However, without submitting the changes first, the Customer did not receive anything.

This little extra step allows you to review, decide, act and then commit all changes with one action. When submitted, Zendesk applies all business rules and can process the ticket. Most of the time, the browser will store your changes in the window, even if you closed the tab by accident. So you might be able to open the tab again and find all your edits. However, don't rely on it. You could lose your changes.

So, update the ticket, pick the proper **Status**, and click **Submit**.

Time for a flowchart

We reviewed a long list of Ticket Statuses used in Zendesk, but there was an essential nugget of information hidden, did you notice? I'm referring to the fact that a ticket can automatically reopen when someone replies to it (it changes from Solved, Pending or On-hold to Open). A ticket's Status can also change even without someone actively changing it.

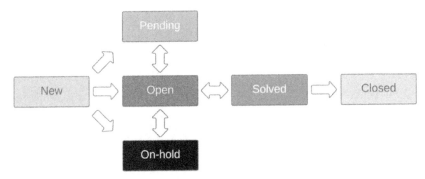

Figure: Lifecycle of tickets.

This chart shows all possible Ticket Statuses in Zendesk. The usual flow is from left to right, New to Closed, with some variations in between. Please note, some arrows are one-way while others are bidirectional.

→ Every ticket starts as a **New** ticket. From here, you can set it to:

- ◆ Open
- ◆ Pending
- ◆ On-hold (if activated by the Administrators)
- ◆ Solved

→ Once you complete your work on an **Open** ticket, you can apply:

- ◆ **Pending** if you want to know something from the Requester
- ◆ **On-hold** if you need information from a third party
- ◆ **Solved** when you consider this ticket done

→ When the Requester replies to a ticket that's **Pending** or **On-hold**, Zendesk changes the Status back to **Open**. This also works if another End User responds, e.g. someone on CC.

→ **Solved** tickets can also be reopened if the Requester or someone else answers with a public comment.

→ A ticket is **Closed** automatically after it has been Solved for four days (by default). It can no longer be reopened (or updated).

This chart demonstrates how the ticket can cycle through different stages. A Customer asks something, and you answer them and then set the Ticket Status to Solved. The Requester replies, which reopens the ticket. You reply and ask if that's all, submitting the ticket as Pending. The Customer confirms it's all good now, and you set the reopened ticket back to Solved. Four days later, a business rule archives the ticket as Closed.

Download the cheat sheet in colour for free[17]

One-touch tickets

By the way, there is no need to go through a whole cycle of back and forth with the Customer. Quite often, a ticket can be immediately set to Solved when providing an answer. We call this a one-touch ticket. You can often achieve this with simple

---

[17] www.nilsrebehn.com/books-zendesk-for-agents-downloads

or straightforward questions (and, of course, if the Agent pays attention and makes sure that the Requester's query is fully addressed).

All that combined can lead to a great Customer experience. A ticket can go from New or Open to Solved without going through another Status. And as long as the user does not reply, it's considered a one-touch ticket.

Follow-up tickets

It's a good thing that Customers can respond to tickets in the Solved state. This reopened ticket allows them to come back to us on the same topic before it's archived (Closed).

Once Closed, it can't be updated or reopened. However, if someone replies to a Closed ticket, a follow-up ticket is created. This ticket is considered New for workflow and reporting purposes, but it references the Closed ticket and imports details into the new ticket. You can work on this ticket like any other ticket and eventually solve it as well.

Tip: Also, at any point, an Agent can change the Status of a ticket to Open, Pending, On-hold, or Solved. There is no need to change any ticket field or leave a comment if it's not necessary. For example, you might want to set a Pending ticket to Solved when you never heard back from the Customer.

Summary

The Ticket Status is an essential system field that indicates where the ticket is in its cycle. It's critical to submit tickets to save all changes and track the appropriate Status. Depending on what happens next, tickets are either reopened or closed for good.

Updating tickets with Macros

When working through a pile of tickets, you end up writing a lot as you help Customers to figure something out or process their requests.

You will likely come across queries that can be answered the same way (for example, the Requester needs to follow the same steps as another user). You might be tempted to copy and paste a text from a previous ticket or a separate text document. Because the comment box is a text editor, you can insert text from another source, of course.

But there is a much better way within Zendesk: it's a feature called **Macro**. It's a set of predefined actions (comments and ticket fields) that updates the ticket. Macros are available on the ticket page, and you can access them via the **Apply Macro** button at the bottom of the page (in the middle).

Screenshot: Choose an available Macro from the list at the bottom of the ticket.

You want to use Macros in situations where a standard response is needed and to save yourself a lot of typing. When you apply a Macro, you have the chance to review the changes before submitting the ticket. Keep in mind that you still need to submit the ticket for any changes to take effect.

Macros are super useful

Macros save us tons of typing. They are especially useful for answering the same kind of inquiries — no need to copy and paste anything from a text file to a ticket.

Macros help us to fill in the same answer repeatedly and standardise our responses. So, for example, you don't need to remember the 15 steps a user needs to do to reset their device and write it each time. Instead, just apply the Macro that explains everything and submit the ticket.

Also, a Macro does not only insert text; it can also update ticket fields. That seems a bit underwhelming at first, but many people underestimate that this is powerful functionality. For example, imagine that a request for a refund comes in: you would need to type a polite reply, assign it to the accounting Group, save it as a Task, and set Priority to Normal. Then select "Refund" from the "Internal ticket category" (custom field) and submit as Open. You can do all that with a Macro with as little as three clicks–without the need to remember all the settings.

Tip: Another thing that's kind of obvious but at the same time isn't—you can apply more than one Macro to a ticket. Where might that be useful? Envision someone sending more than one question in the same ticket, let's say two. You can apply the first Macro that answers the first question (e.g. where to find the past orders in his account) and then apply the Macro that covers the second question (e.g. how to request a partial refund for one of the items on his latest purchase). If you use the Macros in that order, the second comment is inserted below the first one. So there you go: one ticket, two issues quickly addressed.

We will cover how to create your custom Macros a little bit later. But, first, let's practice how to apply some standard Zendesk Macros to tickets.

Other ticket options

Besides Macros, Zendesk has a range of default options an Agent can choose from. You can find a drop-down above the ticket comments. When you click on the down-arrow to open it, you'll see the following options:

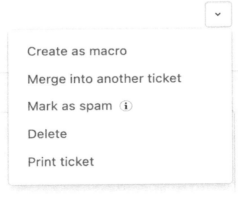

Screenshot: Ticket options

- **Create as macro** opens the Macro editor. We'll cover that in detail in the chapter *Creating your own Macros*.

- **Merge into another ticket*** can be used to combine two tickets into one. For example, if the same user submitted two tickets about the same topic, you might want to merge them. Be careful as this can't be reversed.

- **Mark as spam*** deletes the ticket and suspends the Requester. The user cannot submit new tickets or access your help centre.

- **Delete*** will remove the ticket and place it in **Deleted Tickets,** where you can review and recover them for up to 30 days. We'll cover that in detail in the chapter *Personalising your Views*. The Admins can choose to remove the permission for Agents to merge, delete or mark tickets as spam.

- **Print ticket** opens a printer-friendly window of the current ticket. From here, you can choose to print it on paper or save it as a PDF file–if your browser or computer supports it.

Follow along — Apply a Macro and a Ticket Status (5 minutes)

Let's play through some scenarios to experience how you can use Macros and apply different Ticket Statuses. There are some Macros available in the trial account that we'll use for our practice.

Scenario A

Our first scenario is based on the idea that our support team is jam-packed with support requests. So we'll warn the Customer to expect some delay. It's not the ideal situation, but it can happen in real life. Here it goes:

1) Please **bring up** the previous test ticket *A button on my new keyboard came off.* This is a ticket with one comment from the Requester.

2) **Click** on the **Apply Macro** button at the end of the ticket page (underneath the comments), and you will see a list of available Macros.

3) Look for the Macro **Downgrade and inform**:

   a) Use your cursor to **scroll for and select it**.

   b) Alternatively, **start typing** the word downgrade, and Zendesk shows the Macros containing the characters (or words) you enter here.

4) Before applying any Macro, you have the chance to **preview it.**

   a) Either **click the preview icon** on the right side of the name or press **Shift + Enter**.

   b) A window will show you what the Macro will do to the ticket.

5) There are several ways of running the Macro.

   a) If you are still in the preview window, you can click **Apply Macro**.

b) If you are back in the list of Macros, you can **select the Macro** with your cursor and **click on it** or **press Enter** to apply the selected Macro.

6) Either way, **Zendesk makes the changes** to the ticket as set up in the Macro. In our example, the Macro does two things:

a) Inserts a **public reply** apologising for the delay.

b) Changes the ticket **Priority to Low**.

7) You can now submit the ticket to save the changes. In this scenario, the recommended Ticket Status is Open. Select **Submit as Open** from the bottom right.

Done. You've saved yourself from typing a dozen words or so and changing a ticket field. The more you use it, the more effortless it will be. Let's look at another example.

Scenario B

In this situation, we will follow up with a Customer we reached out to before but have not heard back from.

1) Please **bring up** the previous test ticket *Mouse not connecting*. You have one comment from the Requester and a public comment from you as the Agent.

2) **Open the list of Macros.**

3) Look for **Customer not responding**. Either type any of those words or find and select it from the drop-down list.

4) **Get a preview** (optional) of the Macro again to see the changes the Macro will make in the ticket. Then click **Apply Macro** from that window.

5) If you don't want to preview the Macro, click on **Customer not responding** from the list, or confirm with **Enter**. Zendesk applies the changes to the ticket.

6) In this example, the Macro does **two things**:

   a) Inserts a **public reply** explaining that we are waiting for the Requester to get back to us.

   b) Changes the **Ticket Status to Pending**.

7) You can now **submit the ticket** to save the changes. Press **Submit as Pending** from the bottom right. Note that the Macro set the **Status Pending** for us already, no need to select it by hand.

Perfect. You've saved yourself from typing two dozen words, and you didn't need to write the Customer's name nor update the Ticket Status. The Macro did it all for you.

Reviewing the Customer

We know a lot about tickets, fields, and Statuses by now. But let's not forget the most important aspect of Customer Support—the Customer.

Zendesk captures information about the Requester and saves it in the user profile. Agents can access these details from within the ticket.

There are occasions when you want to check something or get more context on the Requester. From within the ticket, there are at least two ways to learn more about the user:

- User profile (top left)
- User context (top right)

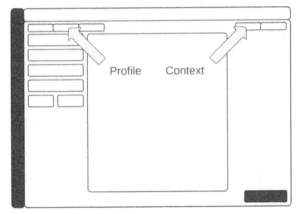

Figure: Access user information

Customer (user) context

This panel is activated by default in a trial account and should be visible on the right-hand side of a ticket. If it's activated but not visible, you can click the button **User** (on the top right of a ticket) to toggle the visibility.

The context panel gives you a high-level view of the Customer. It shows the name, contact details and some other pieces of information Zendesk knows about the user. Underneath, you will find a list of tickets submitted by the same user and other related events. That panel is supposed to give you more context to the Requester's ticket, e.g. you might see another open ticket by the same Customer.

The available information and options on this panel can differ. It depends on the activated channels, extensions, and information available in Zendesk. But in general, it can be a good starting point to get a quick overview.

User profile

In comparison, the user profile is the complete overview of the data we have about that user at any given time. Every user in Zendesk has a profile: End Users, Agents, Admins, etc.

You can access the user profile on the top left part of the ticket. It shows the user name as a tab to the left to the Ticket Number. You can also access a user's profile by searching for their name or email address. We'll cover that later in the chapter about searching in Zendesk.

The focus switches to a new tab within the ticket. We are still on the same ticket but just went to a different layer, so to speak. This tab shows us a range of information.

On the left side of the user profile, you find:

- **Standard fields**
  - User type and role, e.g. End User, Agent, Administrator.
  - Contact details such as email, phone number, and social media alias.
  - Tags (more on that below).
  - Organisation (more on that below).
  - Language, time zone, details, and notes.
- **Custom user fields**
  - Admins can set custom fields for users. They are very similar to ticket fields and offer the same types of data input, e.g. drop-down lists and date fields. User fields come in handy to store Customer information in a standardised form. For example, the Customer's support level or if they have subscribed to the company's newsletter.

In the middle part of the user profile, we have:

- **Profile picture**
  - Most of the time, this is blank for End Users.

- However, Agents can add an image manually to their user profile or via a third party (more on that later).

- **Name**
  - The name is taken automatically from the first ticket that the user submitted. It's either the email alias, phone number, or the channel-specific username (e.g. their Twitter handle).
  - The user's name can be changed manually on their user profile.

- **Tickets**
  - Requested tickets are all the tickets that the user has previously submitted (from New to Closed).
  - CC'd tickets shows all tickets on which they are a CC.

On the top right, you find some actions that you can take:

- **+ New Ticket** creates a new ticket for the user.
- **User options** (Down arrow) provides you access to the following options:
  - Merge into another user. Use this in case there is a duplicate profile for the same user. This gathers all tickets under same user and
  - Suspend access. This disables their login to the help centre and suspends any new requests.

114

○ Delete. This removes the user's account. Agents can only delete users if all their tickets are Closed. Admins can deactivate this option for Agents, so it may not be visible to you.

As you can see, a user profile has a lot of data. That data is either collected automatically when the user is created or is added manually. The profile allows us to get an overview of the ticket history and take some actions on the user or their tickets.

Custom user fields are helpful, but there are two things I want to emphasise related to users: Organisations and Tags.

Organisations

So far, we've spoken about Customers and assumed that they are individuals. Yet, your team might deal with other Customers representing a Group of users (e.g. a company).

An Organisation (Org) within Zendesk is a collection of users under one umbrella. Their use is entirely optional, but gathering them in Orgs allows you to keep track of users and all their requests in one place. This way, your team has a better understanding of all of a company's support requests.

Let's make this more tangible with an example:

Imagine we have an End User called *David*. He is the director of marketing for a fictional company called *Teck Stop*. They have a large number of physical stores where they repair and sell hardware. *Teck Stop* is the biggest reseller for *Berry*, and that makes them an important business partner.

In Zendesk, *Teck Stop* would be an Organisation. *David* would be an End User, and every ticket he ever requested would be associated with his user account. In a hierarchical display, it would look like this:

- Teck Stop (Organisation)
  o David (End User)
    ▪ Ticket 44531

Zendesk stores details for Organisations too. As with users, Organisations have a tab where we can see all the information about them. This tab also comes with standard fields and optional custom fields, much like a user, and you can also access all the Organisation's users and tickets.

Teck Stop's CEO is called *Susan*. In Zendesk, both users are part of the same Org:

- Teck Stop
  o David
    ▪ Ticket 44531
  o Susan
    ▪ Ticket 48411

Whenever *Susan* requests something, her ticket is associated with her user profile. In turn, her profile is connected to the Organisation *Teck Stop*. By accessing the Organisation, any

Agent can see the associated users and all the tickets they requested.

So if *Susan* ever refers to tickets from colleagues like *David*, the Agent can look at the Organisation tab. He'll then discover the other users and their tickets. Setting up organisational structures allows for grouping users together. These structures enable Zendesk to apply rules to many tickets at the same time.

Tags

This brings me to the next topic I wanted to highlight: the use of Tags. Both users and Organisations have Tags as a standard field. Those Tags are pretty much the same as we discussed in the earlier chapter about ticket Tags–they represent extra details that you want to store for later use.

Now the really cool thing (in a geeky way) is that Tags can be **passed down** or inherited by the related object. So if there is one Tag (or more) on a user profile, it (or they) will be **automatically attached** to any ticket created by that user.

For example, *Susan* creates a ticket, and her user profile contains the Tag "vip". The Tag is passed down to the ticket and attached accordingly. So now her ticket, and any other ticket with the same Tag, can be found in Zendesk if someone searches for the Tag "vip".

- Teck Stop
  - Susan (**vip**)
    - New Ticket (**vip**)

The same is true for Tags in Organisations. Zendesk **passes down** any Tag from the Org **to every ticket from any user** in that Organisation. Organisation Tags are not stored or visible in the user profiles, but any ticket created by users in that Organisation will have them automatically attached.

For example, *Teck Stop* is tagged "gold_support", and when *Susan* submits a new question, Zendesk tags that ticket with "vip" **and** "gold_support". That means Zendesk can now trigger any workflow for *VIP* or *Gold-Support* Customers on that ticket.

Now let's assume *David* does not have the "vip" Tag. So if he submits a new query, his ticket will only be tagged with "gold_support". That still sounds fancy, but it doesn't sound as important as *VIP*.

- Teck Stop (**gold_support**)
  - Susan (**vip**)
    - New Ticket (**gold_support, vip**)
  - David
    - New Ticket (**gold_support**)

Any business rules and workflows for *Gold-Support* Customers work for all tickets from *Teck Stop*. However, only *Susan's* tickets get the *VIP* treatment, which could mean that they are routed to a specific Group or View.

Tip: If you remove a Tag from an Organisation or user, the Tag is not removed from any tickets that it has already been added to. If you want to remove Tags from tickets, you have to do it for each ticket manually.

Takeaways

Apart from the geeky bit with the Tags, which I really enjoyed, what do you need to remember from all this? Tickets contain the details of the Customer's query. The user context shows some information about the Customer (the Ticket Requester), and their user profile contains all of the information about them.

Users can be grouped into Organisations. This is entirely optional but useful for some use cases. Also, any Tag attached to Organisations and users will be passed down to tickets, which, in turn, can be used for workflows and business rules.

Moving between tickets

This section of the book is all about working with tickets. So far, we've focused on individual tickets and their components. We know comments, fields, users and Organisations. Once you are done with one ticket, you want to move to the next one.

There are several ways to do this, and in this chapter, we will go into the different options you have within Zendesk. We'll look into tabs, ticket Views, and more.

The dashboard

The first and most basic choice is the dashboard (or home page). You can access it by pressing the Home icon in the navbar. Your trial account will display a **Get started** tab as the first page. You need to click on **Dashboard** to actually open it. In a paid Zendesk account, the Home icon leads straight to the dashboard.

The dashboard shows various elements such as updates to your tickets, tickets assigned to your Groups, the list of tickets requiring your attention, as well as some statistics. It's a great place to start your day, browsing through updates with your first cup of coffee or tea. It's an easy entry point to your first ticket of the day (or after your lunch break). Is there an update on a critical ticket? Do you have open tickets with a high Priority? Click on a ticket and dive straight in.

The ticket Views

In your work as an Agent, the two most important parts of Zendesk are tickets, followed by Views. Naturally, you'll spend the most time on these, and they play a significant role in a typical workday.

Views list tickets based on specific criteria, which is an excellent way of organising and prioritising Customer queries in a list. They can show all unsolved tickets currently assigned to you, or unassigned tickets that need work, or your recently updated tickets. Ticket Views are a great tool to determine what ticket you need to work on next.

Views show up to 30 tickets at a time. If there are more than that in a View, Zendesk shows a pagination element at the bottom of the page so that you can flip through the View page by page, 30 tickets at a time.

CS teams often build Views into their workflows to guide Agents through the ticket queue. For example, the workflow could simply be to address all **New and unassigned tickets** first, then work on **Open tickets** that you are assigned to. Views can also be used to reflect the structure of departments — for example, Customer Service, Accounting, and IT support. Tickets can then be assigned to those teams, and then those Views can be used to help find the respective

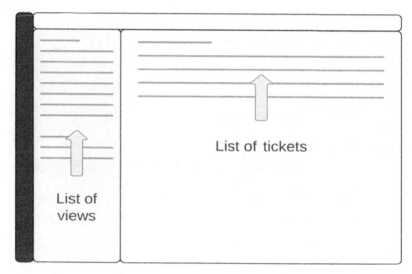

Figure 7: Ticket Views on the left, list of tickets on the right.

Customer queries for that Group. They are very flexible and can cover a lot of different scenarios.

You can access them via the Views icon in the navigation bar on the left. Zendesk lists all the Views that are visible to you on the left and the tickets in the corresponding View on the right. From top to bottom, Views are sorted by the **default** and **shared** Views, followed by **system** Views and finally by the **personal** Views. So what's the difference between these?

- **Default Views** are the set of predefined Views that come with your trial account to help you get started. Some of them are more useful than others. Technically all default Views are shared Views.

- **Shared Views** are Ticket Views that have been set to be visible to all Agents or specific Groups. What the

Agents see and can access can differ. Usually, Administrators are in charge of the default and shared Views. It's pretty common to heavily customise this list and replace the default ones with shared Views.

- **System Views** include Suspended and Deleted tickets. Agents can't edit these.
- **Personal Views** are those that Agents create for themselves. Depending on how Administrators have configured Personal Views, Agents might also be allowed to edit and create Views for Groups.

When working on tickets, you will use Views a lot. Often the name gives you an idea of what kind of tickets are included in a View. You open a View by simply clicking on it.

Zendesk displays the list of tickets in a View sorted by specific criteria, such as the oldest ticket first. They are arranged in a table format, and details are shown in columns such as Subject, Requester, and Priority.

Admins can customise what's shown here, and it usually depends on its purpose. For example, a View called "Open VIP tickets" could display all Open tickets with the Tag "vip", and a View called "Tasks" could list all tickets of the Type task with a column showing the due date.

Screenshot: Select what happens after submitting the ticket.

Next, please

From any View, you can pick a ticket to work on. A common way is to start with the first one on the list. This assumes that the list has been sorted with a purpose, such as the oldest or highest Priority ticket first. After that ticket is processed, you can return to the View to work on the next one.

Or, instead of going back to the list, you could move to the next ticket from within the current tab. After selecting Submit, you can automatically move to the next ticket in the list. To the left of the Submit button, you can choose one of these options:

- **Close the tab** closes the current ticket tab, and goes back to the previous page, e.g. the ticket View.
- **Next ticket in view** moves to the next ticket in the same View.
- **Stay on ticket** keeps you on the current ticket so that you can review the changes or do something else with the ticket.

Using the **next** functionality, you might land on a ticket that's currently being viewed by or worked on by someone else. To better handle these situations, you can use the following feature.

The play functionality

The play mode guides you through the tickets within a given View. You can start it by pressing the Play button on top of the list of tickets when in a View.

After you submit a ticket in play mode, Zendesk moves you to the next ticket in line according to the sorting order, skipping any ticket that another Agent is currently viewing. In addition, The Play mode includes any tickets that are added to the View after you start using it.

For multitaskers

You can work on multiple tickets at the same time. Each ticket opens in a new tab and allows you to review and work on that query. If another ticket requires your attention, you can open it. Then, do what you need to do, submit and close the tab, and return to your previous tab. The browser should store any unsubmitted changes in an open tab for you until you submit the ticket. However, in rare cases, the browser might crash, and you would lose anything you changed in those tabs.

You and I know that this is not really multitasking, as you can only solve one ticket at a time. However, this at least lets you switch between tasks if something else comes up or interrupts you.

Summary

The dashboard might be a good starting point for your work (accompanied by a hot drink of your choice). Views are probably the best starting point to follow a routine. Tabs are for multitaskers and managing interruptions. The Next button and Play allow you to move quickly between tickets without going back to Views. Good stuff, right?

We will cover how to set up Views a little bit later. For now, dive into a follow along practice session for Views.

Follow along — Browsing through tickets (5 to 10 minutes)

If you want to see how you can browse through tickets, you can follow along with the steps below. You'll need at least three tickets in the **All unsolved tickets** View. These are tickets that are neither Solved nor Closed.

Screenshot: Go to Home > Dashboard and then Groups.

126

1) Dashboard
    a) Click the **Home icon** in the navbar on the left (then click **Dashboard** if you are using a Zendesk trial).
    b) Select **Groups** from the top row. A list of your test tickets will show up. These are open tickets in your Groups.
    c) **Open any ticket** from this list.
    d) Write a comment or **apply a Macro**.
    e) **Do not click Submit yet**.
2) Views
    a) Click the **Views icon** in the navbar on the left.
    b) Click the View **All unsolved tickets**.
    c) **Select a ticket** from here that's not already open in a tab.
    d) Write a comment or **apply a Macro**.
    e) **Do not click Submit yet**.

3) Tabs
    a) You should have multiple tabs open. If not, **open another one**.
    b) Next: **go to the previous tab**.
    c) **Observe** how the ticket changes (comment or Macro) are still visible—but not saved because you haven't submitted the changes yet.
4) Next ticket

a) On the current ticket, **select the option Next ticket in view** (left of the Submit button).

b) Update ticket fields or comments e.g. set **Priority to High** and **apply another Macro** at random.

c) **Submit with the Pending Status.**

d) **Zendesk closes this tab,** and you should now see the next ticket.

5) <u>Play mode</u>

a) **Close all ticket tabs** or submit them as Open.

b) Click the View **All unsolved tickets** from the list of Views. Ideally, you have two or more tickets left here. If not, create more test tickets.

c) **Click Play** (on the top right) in that View.

d) Make random changes in ticket fields or comments e.g. set **Priority to Low** and **apply another Macro** at random.

e) The **Next available ticket** option (left to the submit button) should be auto-selected for you.

f) **Submit as Pending.** You should now see the next ticket.

Good. You have now experienced how to move between tickets and work through them efficiently. Which one was your favourite?

Tip: Did you notice how similar **Next ticket in view** and the **Play mode** feel? Yet, underneath there are different mechanics at play. This makes them useful in different situations:

→ The **Next ticket** option lets you work through the tickets in a View in the order you see on screen, top to bottom. After you have updated each ticket in that View, Zendesk stops and goes back to the same View. You go through each ticket once. If another Agent is in the same View, you might end up on the same ticket as the other Agent.

→ With the **Play mode**, you run through a View top to bottom as well. However, you "play" until the View is empty. For example, if you work in **Unassigned tickets**, you go through them until they all are assigned. Likewise, in **All unsolved tickets**, you would cycle through them until all tickets are Solved. If that's not the case, Zendesk will serve you the first ticket on the list again. **Play mode** also avoids Agent collision; it only brings up tickets that no one else has open at the same time.

They are very comparable but helpful in different situations. If you want to check in on all your pending tickets, use the **Next ticket** option (next to the Submit button). This way, you go through the list once, and no other Agent can accidentally end up on the same ticket. When you want to go through all new queries and assign them, you can use **Play mode**, which makes sure that you assign all of them without running into another Agent.

Customising Zendesk For You

Chapters in this section:

- Editing your Agent profile
- Setting photo and signature
- Personalising your Views
- Creating your own Macros
- Understanding where Admins come in

Editing your Agent profile

Every user in Zendesk has a user profile, even you as an Agent, Admin, or Account Owner. Zendesk creates the profile with the role for you when you sign up for a trial version; Admins add other Agents. This profile, like the one for End Users, stores information about you.

Yet, some settings in your profile impact what End Users will see: your name (or alias), profile picture, and signature. Other details are only relevant within the platform, like Groups or Organisations. In this chapter, we'll review the different components. Then, in a later part of the book, we'll go over how to customise your profile.

Access your profile

We are assuming that you are in your trial version or paid version of Zendesk and logged in as an Agent.

You can access your profile from the top bar by clicking on the profile picture icon on the very right end. It might be just a blank generic icon if no picture has been set yet. Then select **View profile** from the drop-down list.

Parts of your profile

You will notice that your profile looks quite similar to that of an End User. Your profile contains:

- Standard fields and user fields on the left.
- Tickets and other settings in the main window.
- **+ New Ticket** to create a new ticket.

Standard fields

You'll find some fields that you're familiar with from End User profiles in the left panel. Others will be new to you. Let's have a closer look at the important parts:

- ❏ **User type and role** define if a user is an End User with few privileges or a Staff member. A Staff member has to have a role associated, e.g. Agent or Admin. Notice that you, as an Agent, can't change your own role. Only users with admin rights can change an Agent's role.

- ❏ **Groups and access** determine what Groups you are assigned to. Each Agent needs to be assigned to at least one Group but can be assigned to several. Only Administrators can change access and Groups for Agents.

- ❏ **Alias and signature** are used for communication. We'll go more in-depth on these when we customise your user profile in another chapter.

- ❏ **Primary email** is your main email address. You can add more addresses here, but your primary email is the only one that receives notifications from Zendesk.

- ❏ **Tags** work similarly to the End Users Tags. Any Tag added to your Agent profile will be attached to the new tickets that you create. They won't be added to tickets you update, though. By default, this is not editable by Agents.

- ❏ **Organisations** can also include Agents. By default, Agents can't change their Organisation.

- ❏ **Language** influences determine the language in which you'd like to view the Zendesk user interface. This setting only affects you.

- ❏ **Time zone** is your local time zone, and any timestamp added to tickets will reflect this, but only on your tickets.

- ❏ **Details and Notes** can provide extra information about your user profile. This is entirely optional and is not used very often.

Any changes you make here are saved immediately.

Tip: You can change your user interface language in your Agent profile, as pointed out above. This is super useful if you want to navigate the system in your preferred language. This change only affects your Agent profile.

If you choose another language from the drop-down list, it's saved instantly, but the browser will still display Zendesk in the previous language. For the change to take effect, you need to refresh your browser. You can refresh most browsers by pressing the [F5] key.

But please note that all descriptions in this book are in English, so it works best if you stick to English for now. You can come back any time to change your language in your Agent profile (and then refresh your browser).

User fields

Any custom user field set up by Administrators will be accessible via the Agent profile as well. However, the field itself might not be applicable at all times. "Support level" or "Company's newsletter" from our examples make little sense for Agents. Those are more relevant for End Users as they might determine the way that their tickets will be treated.

You can ignore the fields that are not relevant to Agents. They can remain blank — just something to bear in mind.

Tickets and other settings

In the main window, you can access your tickets, security settings, and preferences.

- ❑ **Tickets** displays, by default, the tickets that are assigned to you. You can pick another option from the drop-down list. You can see tickets requested by you, followed by you, or where you are CC'd.

- ❑ **Security Settings** allows you to update your password or set up two-factor authentication. You can also make other login related adjustments here.

- ❑ **Preferences** enables notifications from Zendesk. For example, in an incident related to the system, Zendesk will send you an email. This is usually more interesting for Admin who look after the platform itself rather than an Agent.

Tip: Remember these ticket Views in your Agent profile. They allow you to find tickets easily that are hard to find otherwise. For example, suppose you remember that someone added you as a Follower or CC to a ticket, and you want to respond, but you don't recall the Ticket Number. The Views for **Followed tickets** and **CC'd tickets** are your best friends.

New ticket

The only other action that you can take from the main window of your own profile is to create a new ticket. New tickets will be created in your name, meaning you will be the Requester, and you can assign it to others. Use this when you request something that is not related to an existing ticket.

Tip: In a larger company, creating new tickets this way could be used for requesting new hardware from the IT department; or asking the HR team for something. That assumes that those departments are using Zendesk as well. Also, you can create a new ticket using other means and also set yourself as a Requester. It does not need to be created via your user profile.

Summary

Your user profile holds important details such as role and Group. Also, your user interface language setting is "hidden" here. Some of your profile details are set by the system, some by Administrators, while the rest are customised by you.

Setting photo and signature

Some elements from your Agent profile are visible to the Customer when you reply to tickets. We'll have a closer look at what these are, and where to find and how to update them. We will build on the previous chapter, going over the aspects of your Agent profile. By default, you as an Agent have the privileges to edit the following parts.

Your name

The name of your user is on the main window of your profile. Here you see your real name—unless you choose something else during the registration for your trial. This is your user name by which other Agents can find your profile. For example, if someone wants to assign a ticket to you, this name will show up in the list of Assignees.

It will be displayed to everyone in Zendesk. And when you reply to a Customer, this is the name they will see as the sender or person responding—unless you set an alias.

The alias

The alias is a standard user field for Agents. You'll find it in the left panel of the Agent profile. Here you can enter an alternative name, a pseudonym, or a nickname. Or, just your first name instead of your full title of nobility (which might be too hard to spell or too long to read).

Your alias will be shown to End Users when replying to email tickets, posts, and comments. And, if you set an alias, this will be displayed instead of your user name. Leave this blank if you want to use your real (user) name.

People won't be able to find you with your alias within Zendesk (unless your user name and alias is the same, of course).

Tip: If you work in Customer Support, you might not be comfortable sharing your full name. The alias is a good way to mitigate this and protect your privacy. Check with your company's policy on what is allowed or recommended to use. I've seen the alias being used to create a more personal experience using just first names. Some companies or CS teams prefer it this way or for a more technical reason–such as an unusual or difficult name.

Profile photo

Next to your user name in the main window of your Agent profile, you can set your profile photo. Other Agents can see this in Zendesk and End Users in email notifications and when you leave comments in the Zendesk help centre.

Based on my experience, I can highly recommend using a good picture here. It can create a better, more personal experience for the Requester. But check with your company regarding any policies here. Some teams use neutral avatars or just a company logo.

Tip: Your profile picture will be set (and overwritten) if you have a Gravatar[18] account. This is a service linked to WordPress. Users can upload photos there to use as an avatar across several platforms. However, a profile picture set in Gravatar will override the one you load into Zendesk; this can lead to confusion.

Your signature

The signature is another standard user field in the Agent profile. It's an excellent way to personalise your response to email tickets. It adds extra information to every comment in email tickets. The content of the signature field is added to your public ticket comments by default. It becomes the closing line of your comment, but it's not visible in the editor while updating a ticket.

However, Admins can change this behaviour: they can install an account-wide standard signature that replaces the individual Agent signatures. In that case, the content of the signature field won't matter. If you work in a company, check with your team for guidelines on this.

Takeaways

Your user profile determines what End Users see of your identity. You, as an Agent, have control over what they see,

---

[18] See bibliography on page 246

but your company might have a policy or guidelines on what to use. Signatures and photos might be overruled or hidden by the Administrator.

Follow along — Update your Agent profile (5 to 10 minutes)

You'll need your Agent profile for this exercise and a photo to use as a profile picture (a square 1:1 image works best). Make sure you are logged in as your **Agent user**.

First, check how your identity appears out of the box

1) **Create a new test ticket**:

    a) Set your **Agent as the Requester**.

    b) It's essential **not to use** customer@example.com as we want to look at the email notifications you will receive.

2) Enter a **subject**:

    Your order is on its way

3) Then **add a public comment**:

    Hello dear customer,

    Great news, your order is on its way.

    Best Regards

4) **Submit as Pending**.

5) **Open your email inbox** and review the email notification you received as the Requester.

    a) Notice the name of the sender.

b) See how the profile picture and signature looks (they will be blank by default)

The email notification should be straightforward (and relatively plain). So let's improve it a bit.

Customise your name, signature and profile picture

6) **Open your profile**

 a) Click on the **profile icon** on the top right of the page.

 b) Select **View profile** from the drop-down.

 c) Find the name of your user—and leave it as is (that's the name in the main window of your Agent profile). If you followed my examples, it's either **Firstname Agent** or **Tom**.

7) **Set an Alias**

 a) On your Agent profile, **find the alias field on the left**.

 b) Enter something very different from your user name. If you can't think of something creative, just use your **first name** instead (without the word Agent) or enter your full name. Just make sure it's different from your actual user name in the main window.

 c) **Move** the cursor to the **signature field** on your profile.

 d) **Notice that the changes are saved** immediately, so no need to click anything else.

8) **Set a signature**

   a) **Enter a fictional signature here**. Notice that this is a multi-line field, which means that you can enter several rows of text. Here you can enter a farewell message and then your name and a company name in the paragraph underneath. For example:

   Thanks and regards,

   Tom

   Berry Ltd - your first choice in computer peripherals.

   b) Again, as soon as you **move to another field**, the changes are saved.

9) **Upload profile picture**

   a) **Click the profile icon** next to your user name on your profile.

   b) Select **Upload a new photo**.

   c) **Pick an image from your computer**. Ideally, a photo with a 1:1 aspect ratio, anything else will

look distorted. Think of the square format that's used on Instagram.

Screenshot: Customise your alias, signature and profile picture.

Next, we'll check how the email notification looks now:

10) Go back to the **previous test ticket**.

    a) **Add a public comment**:

        Dear customer,

        Your order is around the corner. It will be delivered today!

    b) **Submit as Pending**.

11) Then **review the email notification** you received as a Requester.

    a) Notice the name of the sender is now **your alias**.

    b) See how the **profile picture** shows up next to your alias.

    c) Check out the **signature at the end of the comment**.

Looks much better, right? Even if not, hopefully, it's clear what impact your changes have on the notifications.

Personalising your Views

The Zendesk user interface has specific areas that Agents can customise. Agents can edit some things; Admins can edit the rest. One of these places is the ticket Views. They are one of the most critical aspects of an Agent's daily routine. And that's why we'll focus on personalising them.

You can find them in the navigation bar on the left. It shows all Views available to you depending on your role or the Group(s) you belong to. The trial account comes with a range of default Views (that are shared amongst all users). The system Views (for suspended and deleted tickets) are set up in every Zendesk by default. Below that, the system will list all your personal Views (there are no personal Views out of the box).

In a previous chapter, we covered how to work with tickets and learned how to utilise Views in various ways. But how do Views work? How does Zendesk determine what tickets to include in what View?

Views are basically filters

Think of Views as filters—not folders or an inbox. Zendesk is not like an email tool. For example, you can't move a ticket to a View like you would move a message into a folder. Instead, you assign a ticket to a Group or person, which determines where a ticket shows up. That also means that a ticket can be visible in multiple Views.

Looking at them as a way to filter through tickets is the best explanation I can think of. Even Zendesk referred to them as filters at one point. If you go to any View in Zendesk and check the URL, you'll notice it says ...Agent/filters/...

Tip: You can use those specific URLs to bookmark individual Views. These make it easier to skip the dashboard and jump straight to your most-used View.

Views show tickets based on specific criteria that you define. The View called **Your unsolved tickets** shows you tickets assigned to you and not Solved (or Closed) yet. **Unassigned tickets** show you tickets that are not assigned to anyone (and not Solved or Closed) yet.

When you log in and have a look at the default Views in your Zendesk, you might see the following distribution (this is an example):

- Your unsolved tickets (15)
- Unassigned tickets (45)
- All unsolved tickets (120)

Your unsolved tickets shows all tickets assigned to you that are not Solved (or Closed) yet. That can be tickets that are either Open, Pending, or On-hold. In our example, It's 15 in total for now.

Unassigned tickets are not assigned to anyone and are neither Solved nor Closed. This filter does not include the tickets from the previous View because this View shows unassigned tickets only. After the weekend it went up to 45.

All unsolved tickets show all tickets across the team in any state less than Solved or Closed. This View includes your tickets, unassigned tickets, and every ticket from everyone else. Right now, it's 120 in total.

Of these 120 tickets: 15 are assigned to you, 45 are not assigned to anyone, and 60 are assigned to other Agents–all of them not Solved yet. Note that unassigned tickets and those assigned to you show up in the different Views and in **All unsolved tickets**. That is because of the criteria of this View.

You might wonder why it's useful that tickets show up in more than one View. The previous example would allow you to work on your tickets first (Your unsolved tickets) and then move to New tickets in your team (Unassigned tickets). The View for all tickets (All unsolved tickets) allows you and your team to access everyone's tickets. That is useful when team members need to help each other out. Also, it can indicate how big the ticket backlog is.

Shared Views

All of the default Views in your trial are shared with everyone. Meaning any Agent has access to any of them. This is a common setting for Views in a team, and only Administrators can change that.

System Views

There are two Views in every Zendesk that can't be edited: Suspended tickets and Deleted tickets.

Suspended tickets show tickets that are unwanted for one reason or another. There is a range of reasons; the most common one is that they are either spam, an automated notification from another system, or messages from a suspended user. It's only visible to Agents that can access all tickets.

Deleted tickets are all tickets that have been deleted in the Zendesk account. It's like the trash bin on your computer desktop. Tickets stay here for 30 days before they are permanently deleted. However, by default, it's only visible to Administrators.

Personal Views

Personal Views are also called custom Views. Agents create them for personal use. By default, this privilege is activated, but Admins can deactivate it. The visibility of (or access to) these Views is limited to yourself.

Components of a View

You now know where to find and how to use Views. You learned about the different kinds and when to use them. Now we'll zoom into Views and take a look at their components.

You can create Views from the Admin section (Admin > Manage > Views > Add view). Here are all the components of a View:

- **Name** is required for every View–that's how they appear in the list of Views. Ideally, the name is descriptive, such as "Recently updated tickets" or "Pending tickets".

- **Description (optional)** allows other people to understand the View's purpose. However, it's only visible in the admin section and not the list of Views.

- **Access** determines the visibility of a View. For example, Admins can make Views available to all Agents–or Agents in specific Groups, which turns it into a shared View. In addition, Agents and Admins can set up Views for themselves, which is then considered a Personal View.

- **Conditions** are the criteria by which you can filter tickets. We will cover them in more detail below.

- **Formatting** options allow you to set the columns that are displayed in a View. Most ticket fields and other ticket information are available to add as a column. Imagine a spreadsheet with table headers where you'll define what to see in what column. You can add up to

10 columns and change the order via drag and drop. The Ticket Status is always visible to the left of the ticket data columns.

- **Sorting options** allow you to group tickets, e.g. by Status or Priority, and then order them by date or Ticket ID.

Filter tickets with conditions

The filter conditions are the essential component of a View. Let's cover them in detail to see how they can be used in Views. These criteria are almost exclusively based on what's available in the ticket.

System fields include the ticket's Status, its Priority, and Type (for example, "Status is New" or "Priority less than High"). The operators "less than" and "more than" help to include more than one option.

Custom fields such as drop-down and checkbox fields are supported in Views (for example, "Product category is DSLR cameras").

Tags filter tickets for specific Tags. Either they include one Tag (or several) or do not have one (or several Tags) attached to them (For example, "Tags contain none of the following gold support").

Description is the content of the ticket. This condition checks for the first comment (not including the subject line) of a ticket. You can use operators to look for specific words (or phrases) and either include or exclude them.

Ticket criteria such as channel or email address can be used to select specific tickets (for example, "Channel is Email" will show all tickets that came in via email).

Time-based conditions are based on the hours that have passed since the last update (for example, add Hours since created, Hours since Pending, etc.).

Requester and Assignee allow you to filter for the Requester or Agent. This includes individual Agents or a specific Organisation. Remember when we covered *Teck Stop* as an example? You could build a View that only includes tickets from *Teck Stop*. This is useful in situations when you need to know who submitted a ticket.

The All and Any operators

You control what appears in Views by using the **All** and **Any** operators. Once you know the conditions that you want to use, you need to decide what operator to use. In other words, you are building a small formula:

All of these conditions + **Any** one of the following conditions Suppose that you want to see tickets that are New and have a High Priority. You would use Status is New and Priority is High and put both of those conditions in the **all** section. The emphasis here is on *and*. Both conditions need to be true.

The other operator is **any**. Use this if one of the conditions should be true. For example, let's assume a View should show tickets about DSLR cameras or Film cameras (custom ticket field). You would set the conditions as follows: the Product category is DSLR cameras, or the Product category is Film cameras—the emphasis is on *or*. You would put these conditions in the **any** section because one of the conditions needs to be true.

And, you can actually combine all and any conditions. For example, you want to display New tickets with the Priority High for the DSLR and Film cameras. The conditions are: Show all tickets where the Status is New and Priority is High, plus, where the Product category is "DSLR cameras" or "Film cameras".

In the View editor, that would look like this:

→ Meet **all** of the following conditions

  ◆ Status is New

  ◆ Priority is High

→ Meet **any** of the following conditions

  ◆ Product category is DSLR cameras

  ◆ Product category is Film cameras

Zendesk would make sure both conditions on top (*all of the following*) are valid. And one of the criteria below (*any of the following*) is true.

Figure: Setting the All and Any conditions in Views.

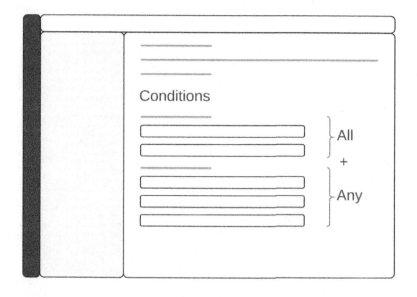

Limitations

By default, Agents can only set up and edit Views for themselves, not for other Agents. However, Administrators can change these privileges on certain Zendesk plans.

There is only limited space in the list on the left panel. Zendesk will display up to 12 shared Views (plus the system Views) and a maximum of 8 personal Views underneath. You can have more Views than that, but you can only access them by clicking the **More** option at the bottom of the list.

Tip: I recommend thinking about how to use the limited space for Views. What tickets do you need to see? Does another View already include them? Can you combine several Views into one by being clever with the configuration? Place your most valuable or essential filters at the top of the list so that you can access them quickly.

Common questions answered

When to use personal Views

Use personal Views when the shared Views do not include the tickets you need to see regularly.

I'm an Agent and can't add Views

Every Agent can add and edit personal Views for themselves but not add or edit shared Views. If you don't have the option to add personal Views, that option has been deactivated by the Administrator.

Recap

Views are great tools for the Agents. You can set them up for personal use but not be limited to just *your* tickets (assigned to you). Views act like filters; you can define criteria to cut through a vast amount of tickets. All and any operators allow you to put together some powerful formulas for viewing just the tickets you want to see. Use them wisely.

Follow along — Personal Views (15 minutes)

Please log in as an Agent to follow along. First, we'll explore an existing View, clone it, and then set up a total of three personal Views.

Personal View A: **All Open tickets**

The View **Your unsolved tickets** filters all tickets assigned to you with the Status New to Pending. However, when you want to reply to Customers, you only want to see New and Open tickets. So we'll set up a View for that.

1) Go to the **Admin section** (click on the gear icon in the navbar).
2) Select **Manage > Views** to see a list of active Views.
3) Click **Clone view** for **All unsolved tickets**.
4) On the next page, change the name to **All Open tickets** (at the very top of the tab).
5) **Enter a description** (optional).
6) Who has access: **Only you** (that's the only option you have at the moment).

7) Under conditions, you will see **Status less than Solved**. Change it to **Status less than Pending**. This way, it displays only tickets with the Status New and Open. Refer to the chapter <u>Applying Status to tickets</u> to see all available Ticket Statuses again.

8) **Leave the other settings** as is and scroll down the page.

9) Click **Save**. Similar to tickets, changes on this page are only saved if you choose to save them.

10) Zendesk shows you a list of all **shared Views** again.

11) Click on **All shared Views** and change it to **Personal Views**. You will now see all your personal Views. From here, you can open, edit, and clone them.

12) **Open the list of Views** by clicking the View icon in the navigation bar on the left.

13) Click the **refresh** button for Views (the little circle right next to the word Views).

14) Notice how the new entry appeared at the bottom under **Your Views**. Select it to open and inspect your New and Open tickets.

Personal View B: **My old tickets**

After you have worked on many tickets, you will have quite a few tickets with the Status Pending. These are tickets that are waiting for a reply from the Requester. If you're waiting too long for a response, you might want to follow up with them. Let's build a View for that.

1) Go to the **Admin section** (click on the gear icon in the navbar).

2) Select **Manage > Views**.

3) Click **Add view**.

4) On the next page, enter the name **Older tickets**.

5) **Enter a description** (optional).

6) Who has access: **Only you**.

7) Under **all** conditions, **add these**:

   a) **Status is Pending**.

   b) **Assignee is current user**. This condition ensures that the View displays only tickets assigned to you.

   c) **Hours since update Greater than 48**. This represents the number of calendar hours since the last update. Forty-eight hours would equal two calendar days, no matter if there is a holiday or a weekend.

8) You should now have **three conditions** in **all**. Click **Preview**.

a) Zendesk will run through the conditions and show you **up to 15 tickets** that meet the criteria. It also shows you how many tickets there would be in total if you save the View. Since this is a test account, you might not have many or any tickets at all to display.

b) **If it does not show any tickets**, you might want to reduce the number of **Hours since update Greater than to 1** to get a result. Of course, you wouldn't follow up with most Customers in real life after just one hour, but this way, you should see at least some tickets in this preview.

9) **Scroll down** to the **formatting options**.

    a) Find the column for **Satisfaction** and remove it by clicking **X**.

    b) **Add column** and choose the **Latest update** from the list.

    c) Leave **Group by** as **No group.**

    d) Go to **Order by** and select **Latest update** from the drop-down list.

    e) Tick the radio box next to **Ascending**.

    f) Click **Save**.

10) **Go to Views** via the navigation bar.

    a) Click the **refresh** button for Views.

    b) Have a look at your View **Older tickets**.

    c) Inspect the columns, look for **Updated**, and notice how they are sorted by the oldest updates first.

    d) It's ok if you **don't see any tickets** in this View. This means you don't have tickets that meet the criteria. However, it's a helpful View to have when you start working with Zendesk.

Personal View C: **Important tickets**

The following example builds on the idea that you have *important* tickets. Meaning that they are from important Customers or have a higher Priority for some reason. This assumes we have some tickets with the Tag **gold_support** or with the **Priority High** or **Urgent**. You might want to create a handful of test tickets for this to follow along.

1) Go to the **Admin section** (click on the gear icon in the navbar).
2) Select **Manage > Views**.
3) Click **Add view**.
4) Enter **Important Open tickets** as the name.
5) **Enter a description** (optional).
6) Who has access: **Only you**.
7) Under **all** conditions, add **Status less than Solved**.
8) Under **any** conditions, add **Priority greater than Normal**.
9) Also, under **any** conditions, add **Tags contains at least one of the following gold_support**.
10) Click **Preview**. If you have New or Pending tickets assigned to you with High or Urgent Priority or the vip Tag, you should see them now.
11) **Scroll down** to the **formatting options**.
    a) **Remove** the column for **Satisfaction**.
    b) **Add** a column for **Priority** and drag it to the **first position**.

c) Go to **Group by** and select **Priority** from the drop-down list in **descending order**.

d) Click **Save**.

12) **Open Views** via the navbar and refresh the list.

a) **Open your new View** and have a look at the tickets in the list.

b) The tickets are bundled (or **grouped**) with their respective Priority, from highest to lowest Priority.

By the way, this third View shows tickets assigned to any Agent, not just you. It demonstrates that personal Views can also be used for tickets that are assigned to other Agents. This example helps you to find important tickets that need a reply, no matter who they are assigned to.

If you have several custom Views, you might want to change the order they appear in the side panel.

1) Go to **Admin > Manage > Views**.

2) Switch from Shared Views to **Personal Views**.

3) Click **Reorder page** (next to Add view).

4) **Drag and drop** the Views in the order you like.

5) Click **Save**.

I prepared some templates for these (and more) Views. You, as a reader, can download them from my website for free[19] .

---

[19] www.nilsrebehn.com/books-zendesk-for-agents-downloads

Creating your own Macros

Agents work on a ton of tickets, and you can typically solve many of them in a similar way. Macros help you to repeat the same actions on these similar tickets. In addition, you can combine several ticket updates into one, including canned responses. For teams, Macros are set up by Administrators and then shared with Agents. However, you can also create your own personal Macros.

Here we cover how to create them.

Create Macros from tickets

You already learned how to find and apply Macros from within a ticket. However, you can also create a new Macro from the ticket you are currently viewing, which is handy when you want to create a standard action (or reply) for something you often encounter.

To do this, you need to be on a ticket and select **Create as Macro** from the list of actions. Then, Zendesk opens the Macro editor page and copies over most settings from the ticket page. These include ticket fields and Tags and, if you have left a comment, the comment text as well.

We will cover how to create a Macro in this way in a practical exercise later.

Build your own Macros

You can also create Macros from the Admin section (Admin > Manage > Macros > Add Macro). If you add a new Macro this way, Zendesk will not pre-set anything. Either way, if you create a Macro from a ticket or from scratch, the following components are the same:

- **Name** is how you find it in the list of Macros.
- **Description** can be a few words describing what the Macro does. It can help you to remember when you look at it later. This is optional.
- **Availability** determines who can view and use the Macros. Agents can typically only create Macros for themselves.
- **Actions** are where you define the steps Zendesk should take when you apply the Macro to a ticket. You add actions here, and they will all be applied to the ticket. Just avoid duplications. For example, if you set the Priority to Normal and High in the same Macro, one will overwrite the other. Zendesk will apply the actions in the order defined in your Macro. For example, if you've set Priority to High and then further down in the list of actions you set it to Normal, the Macro will apply the Normal Priority.

Since there are many actions available, we'll look at some of them more closely.

Available actions in Macros

I would categorise actions into two areas: Text actions and actions for ticket fields:

Text actions

- **Subject** sets (and overwrites) the subject of a ticket. Most of the time, you want to leave the subject as is. But there might be some workflows where this helps to sort the tickets.

- **Comment mode** determines if the comment added by this Macro is public or private. It only takes effect if you actually add a comment as an action. If you don't set this, the comment will be public. But, even if you want to apply a public comment, I would still recommend setting this, just to make sure that it's visible to End Users.

- **Comment** is the text you add as a comment to the ticket. With the action comment mode (above), you can define if this comment is public or private. You can write hundreds of words and format them as well.

- **Placeholders** are predefined variables and allow you to place data from Zendesk into your comments. For example, you can use placeholders for the name of the Requester and the Ticket ID. Then, when the Macro is applied, Zendesk replaces the placeholder with the data that is specific to the ticket, user and Org. See an example in the exercise later.

Ticket field actions

- **People** actions allow you to set the Group or individual Assignee the ticket should be assigned to. You can also add a Follower if you want.
- **System fields** to set Type, Priority, and Status as an action.
- **Tags**
    - **Add Tags** will add new Tags to the existing ones already on the ticket.
    - **Set Tags** will **remove all Tags** and replace them with the ones you define here.
    - **Remove Tags** will remove one or several Tags you specify here.

    Tip: I rarely see the **Set Tag**-action being used or where it can be helpful. In most cases, you want to keep Tags on tickets or only remove specific ones. Given that it replaces all Tags, I would recommend not using it and only using **Add Tags** or **Remove Tags**.

- **Custom fields** are custom drop-down and checkbox fields you can set with Macros.

Tip: Since you can add text to tickets via Macros, it's tempting to add a signature at the end. I would advise against it. Imagine you set up 20 Macros, and you want to update your signature. Maybe you want to change some words or update

165

a phone number or website address. To do that, you would need to go to each Macro and make the changes. That's what your signature field on the Agent profile is for.

Organise your Macros

If you have more than a handful of Macros, it might be worth spending a couple of minutes organising your Macros. The Macros page (Admin > Manage > Macros) lists all Macros that you have access to. In addition, you can filter for shared Macros and personal Macros, active and inactive ones.

The order in which they appear here defines the order in the list of available Macros on a ticket. You can reorder them manually or have Zendesk sort them alphabetically.

From here, you can also search, edit, clone, deactivate, and delete Macros.

Cloning can be useful if you want to set up a lot of similar Macros. And when it comes to deleting, I would recommend deactivating a Macro rather than deleting it. If you delete one, it's gone for good. But if you deactivate it, you can reactivate it (or clone it) later.

Tip: You can also categorise your Macros to bundle up similar or related Macros. This way, it's easier to apply or organise them. However, it's more of a hidden option as there are no apparent settings in the user interface.

You categorise Macros by formatting the title with two colons (::) between the different levels or folders you want to create. So, for example, if you name a Macro **Escalate::Support Level**

2, it would show up as a folder called **Escalate** with **Support Level 2** as an option. I will show you this in more detail in an exercise later.

Common questions answered

<u>When to use personal Macros</u>

In most companies, Administrators, managers, or team leads define Macros and their availability. They decide what Macros the team or Groups need and which are relevant to them. Those Macros should cover the most common ticket types, questions, and use cases. In a good setup, they cover almost everything.

If shared Macros do not cover something you need or need specific Macros for your unique workflow, personal Macros can fill the gap.

In smaller teams, it's expected that individual Agents take care of many different questions from Customers. As a result, those Agents are likely to create Macros for their daily work. Admins should help Agents share those Macros amongst the team; shared Macros allow for a standardised and efficient way of working.

<u>What to do if you can't set personal or shared Macros</u>

Administrators can take away the privilege to create personal Macros. There might be a policy in place in your company that prevents that.

Then there might be the case where you can create personal Macros and want to share them with the team. In some teams, it's common practice to discuss new Macros and share them with the team. An Admin or a team lead often facilitates this. It's a good practice to review and update shared Macros regularly. That's often part of regular team meetings. Outdated Macros are either retired (deactivated) or updated. This can also be the place to talk about Macros that are not available yet. If you have an excellent personal Macro that can be useful for the rest of the team, you can make it available to the rest of the Group or company.

Wrap up

Macros are a powerful tool for Agents and Admins alike. They help a lot when the same thing needs to happen on several tickets, again and again. Agents can choose the best Macro for a situation and avoid typing the same stuff over and over. Macros can also update ticket fields and add information where required. For these reasons, use them to your advantage.

Follow along — Personal Macros (10 minutes)

Please log in as an Agent to follow along. First, we'll create a Macro from a ticket and then from scratch.

Create a Macro from a ticket

1) Open any of your **test tickets**.
2) **Add a Tag,** e.g. **test**.
3) Write a **comment,** anything you want.
4) Submit as **Open**, but **stay on the ticket.**
5) Then open the drop-down on the top right (above the ticket comments) to see the available actions. Select **Create as Macro.**
6) On the page for the new Macro, enter the name **Internal Update.**
7) **Enter a description** (optional). This is what shows up on the Macro-preview.
8) Available for: **Me only** (is the only option for now).
9) Review the actions.
   a) If you see **Assignee**, remove it.
   b) If you see **Type**, remove it.
   c) Look for **Group** and make sure to select one, e.g. **Support.**
   d) Find the **comment mode**, change it to **Private.**
   e) Under **Comment/description**, change the text to this:
      Please have a look at this.
   f) Click **Create.**

10) Open any **test ticket**.

11) **Refresh** the browser:

    a) **Ctrl + R** at the same time (on Windows).

    b) **Command + R** (on Mac).

12) Go to **Apply Macro** and select **your Macro** from the list.

13) Check out the **Preview** (optional).

14) **Apply the Macro**.

15) Zendesk executes all the actions in your Macro on the current ticket. **Review** if everything looks as planned.

16) Click **submit,** and you are done.

Create a Macro from scratch

1) Go to **Admin > Manage > Macros** and click **Add Macro** (on the top right).

2) On the page for the new Macro, **enter the name Escalation::Admins**. Notice the double colon (::); this creates Macro categories.

3) **Enter a description** (optional).

4) Under actions, **add Priority** and select **High**.

5) Add **Assignee** and select your **Admin user**. Remember, you are currently logged in as the Agent. This step simulates the ticket assignment to someone other than yourself.

6) Add a **Comment/description**:

    This is an important ticket and needs your attention:

7) Add the following two **placeholders**:

{{ticket.title}}

{{ticket.url}}

8) Add **comment mode** and choose **Private**.

9) Select **Add Tags** from actions. Make sure it's Add Tags and not Set Tags. Add a Tag of your choice, e.g. **escalation**.

10) Click **Create**.

11) Go to a **test ticket**.

12) **Refresh** the browser.

13) Go to **Apply Macro** and select **your new Macro** from the list.

14) Look for your Macro and notice how it's **nested in another folder**. That is the Macro category. It's **categorised as Escalation**, and from there, you can apply it.

15) Zendesk will execute all the actions in your Macro. **Review** if everything looks as planned.

16) Click **submit**.

I prepared some templates for these (and more) Macros. You, as a reader, can download them from my website for free[20].

---

[20] www.nilsrebehn.com/books-zendesk-for-agents-downloads

Tip: In this scenario, we use the assign action to assign a ticket directly to another Agent or Admin. Usually, I would not recommend assigning to an Agent directly. However, we do it here because the trial account has a limited number of users and Groups.

Outside a test environment, it's better to assign to a Group rather than one person. Even if you know that he or she is the go-to person for this kind of ticket, there are still advantages to assigning it to the Agent's Group instead. Because if that person is not working today or this week, the ticket will not get the attention it requires.

Instead, when you assign it to a Group, someone else can pick it up and work on it. So in the scenario above, we would have a Group called *Admins* or *Managers* and assign it to one of those Groups. Then there would be a good chance that someone in the Group will work on it.

Of course, it always depends on the size of the team that works in Zendesk. But, it's worth keeping that in mind.

Configuring Zendesk as Admin

The section on customising your Zendesk was the most "technical" part of this book. We were updating the Agent profile and creating Views and Macros. We covered detailed settings "behind the scenes". The average Agent spends most of their time on tickets and helping Customers, not making configuration changes to Zendesk.

You might have noticed what's available on your Admin page when logged in as an Agent. It's limited to personal settings, and they are very useful to customise your workspace.

Administrators can also change Views and Macros, and they would do that on a team or account level. On top of that, they can access all the other features. The most powerful features are automated business rules and reporting. The Admin role in Zendesk allows you to change everything an Agent can't.

In some companies, this job goes to the IT department. In others, it goes to someone else outside Customer Service. But often, this role stays within the CS department—and I think this is a good idea. This way, changes can be implemented faster, without going through another team.

Larger organisations will have dedicated personnel looking after their Zendesk. However, in many mid-sized businesses, the role of the Administrator falls into the hands of the CS manager. You will find many teams that will use hybrid functions, where an Admin solves tickets for the most part but can make changes to Zendesk when necessary. Sometimes they are referred to as a super-user, someone that is very experienced in his field.

In the remaining sections, we will cover productivity tips and an Agent's typical workday. Still, you can check out my other resources if you want to learn more about Zendesk administration[21].

---

[21] www.nilsrebehn.com/books-zendesk-agents-to-admins

Productivity Tips

Chapters in this section:

- Searching efficiently
- Updating multiple tickets
- Using shortcuts in Zendesk
- Extending Zendesk via apps
- Solving tickets on the go

Searching efficiently

Views are handy for finding tickets where you expect them to be, but there will be times when you'll need to look for tickets that are not available in your Views. For example, a colleague could ask you to take a look at a particular ticket, or you need to find a specific user or all of an Organisation's tickets.

That's when the Zendesk-wide search comes in handy. You can search for tickets, users, Organisations, and articles in your help centre. Agents will find everything they have permission to see. By default, you can search for everything, but some companies might have policies that restrict visibility. In that case, Administrators might allow visibility to only tickets in your Groups or assigned to you.

Search for tickets

You can access the general search in a few ways. One is via the **+Add** tab in the top bar. Hover over it, then select **Search** from the drop-down. A blank search page will appear in the main window.

Another way is via the search icon in the top bar on the right. Click on the magnifying glass to open the search field, insert one or more words, then press enter. The result will appear on the search page in the main window.

Either way, Zendesk opens a new tab for the search page. That means you can always switch between this tab and other tabs you might have open.

If you open the search page via the **+Add** button, the page shows no results. Instead, you need to enter your search terms and press enter to get any results. The second approach opens the page with the results for your search term. That's why I prefer (and recommend) the second way. It's much quicker.

Tip: If you enter a Ticket Number in the search box (and press enter), Zendesk will go straight to that specific ticket. It will not show you the results page but will open a separate ticket tab related to that Ticket ID.

What you can search for

After you enter a search term (a word or combination of words or characters entered into a search engine to specify a particular thing to be searched for), Zendesk lists the results. The results page shows you tickets, users, and Organisations. If you have help centre articles, it will display relevant Zendesk Guide Articles as well. There might be more tabs available subject to the Zendesk version in use.

The list will show results split into several tabs. The **Tickets** tab shows the ID (Ticket Number), subject, and other details. The **Users** and **Organisations** tabs list the names and additional available information. Finally, the **Articles** tab lists all items in your help centre that match the search.

You can browse the results and jump straight to the Ticket, User, Org, or Article by clicking on it.

One more thing: Zendesk only shows the first 1,000 results of a search. 1,000 is too much to browse through anyway. Even a hundred tickets can take a while to go through. That's when it's helpful to filter the results.

Filter search results with... filters

On the results page, you have the option to filter the list. You can limit it to Tickets, Users, Organisations, or Articles only. Filter for one or several Ticket Statuses, Types, or Tags. You can also filter for the Assignee and the latest update date (or date range).

Every time you add or remove a filter, Zendesk updates the search results. This way, you can narrow down the list and find the droids you're looking for–or tickets, users, etc.

Figure: Add search filters via the drop-down.

Tip: There is a way to *save* your search. You can press **Copy link** next to the filter selection to copy the URL of this search to the clipboard. Then you can save it as a bookmark or share it with another Agent.

What if you find yourself running a search on a specific kind of ticket over and over? Saving a search is one way to find particular tickets again. But, if you frequently search for the same type of tickets, I recommend creating a personal View– they offer similar filter criteria (and more) and are easily accessible. You can also access those tickets from your list of Views whenever needed. If you are looking for these specific tickets, others might be as well. So, tell your Zendesk Admin about your View, and they can turn it into a shared View if it's helpful for others.

Filter search results with... operators

Narrowing down search results with the available filters is very useful already. They cover the most commonly used searches, and using them is quick and should suffice in most cases. But you can narrow down the results even further.

The keen observer might have noticed them already. When you add criteria via the drop-down filter selection, Zendesk adds words into the search bar. So, for example, when you search for the word **refund** and choose **Status Open** from the filter drop-down, Zendesk adds **Status:Open** to the search– this is a search operator.

Zendesk adds those operators for you when you use the built-in filters. The user interface makes it easy for you to insert operators without remembering any of them. But, it limits you to the options from the list.

You can also enter operators by hand, and there are a whole bunch of them the filter drop-down is not showing you. It's time to bring out the inner geek again.

Ticket properties

❑ You already saw **Status, Type, Tags, Assignee** and **date**.

❑ Other operators allow you to look for **Priority, Requester, Group, channel**. Examples include **Priority:High** (shows tickets with the Priority High) and **Priority>Normal** (for tickets with Priority higher than Normal).

❑ My favourite, and likely the most useful, is for custom fields. Let's assume you have a custom field called *Category*. You can use this operator **category:dslr_cameras**. The results will show tickets where that field value is present.

❑ The **creation date** shows tickets created at a specific date or within a date range. It can be more helpful than the filter for the date of the last update.

User and Organisation properties

❑ A search of Users and Orgs looks for **names** and **email addresses**. But, with operators, you can look for specific **roles** and the content of **notes and details**. You can even search for suspended users.

❏ The **creation date** helps find Users or Organisations created at a specific date or within a date range. For example, created<2029-01-01 shows any User and Org created before January 1st 2029.

Screenshot: Search results with operators.

It goes beyond our scope to explain every search operator. The complete reference[22] is available online. For now, it's enough to know that there are more options than just the default filters.

Search for users only

There is a third way to search, but it shows only users, and it's a bit hidden.

You can find it in the Admin section: go to Admin > Manage > People. The main window shows a search box and a list of users. Here you can see the total number of users in Zendesk that are visible to you as an Agent.

You can start browsing or search for users via the search field provided. Enter anything user-related such as name or email. Search operators for users work here too.

This way of searching users won't be relevant during your day to day as an Agent. But, for completeness' sake, it's worth mentioning.

Recap

That's all about searching in Zendesk. Very straightforward (I hope). The most useful (and quickest) way to search is via the top bar's search field. Remember how to use the built-in filter options. And if you have a knack for it, think of the manual search operators.

---

[22] See bibliography on page 246

Updating multiple tickets

In your daily work, you will come across questions that are similar or somehow related. Either several Customers are asking the same things, or they are reporting the same issues. Of course, Macros can help answer those quickly, but wouldn't it be even better to select and update a bunch of tickets simultaneously?

Zendesk allows you to select many tickets and apply changes to them in one go, without the need to go through them one by one. You can even run Macros across all of them at the same time.

And you can do this from almost anywhere in Zendesk that shows a list of tickets.

Select several tickets

The most logical place to start with is the ticket Views. That's where we have a list of tickets–rows and rows of them. You can select one ticket by clicking the checkbox to the left of the Ticket Status. A little checkmark appears on the left, and Zendesk highlights the whole row in a different colour. From there, you can mark another ticket. Click the checkbox on every ticket that you want to select.

You can also select every ticket in that View. On top of the individual checkboxes (underneath the name of the View), you'll find another checkbox. This box doesn't have any description. If you tick it, Zendesk will select all tickets for you in the current list.

A View shows up to 30 tickets at once. You can select them one by one or all of them at once using that main checkbox on top. If you have more than 30 tickets in a given View, Zendesk breaks it into pages, and a navigation bar at the bottom allows you then to flip to the next page, which also shows up to 30 tickets. Your selection of tickets on the pages stays active; after selecting tickets on one page, you can then select more tickets on other pages.

This works in other places too. You can select tickets in the dashboard, User profiles, Organisations, and search results page. Pretty much every list of tickets in Zendesk allows you to choose more than one (or all) tickets.

Update batches of tickets

After selecting more than one ticket this way, a new button will appear on the top right that says **Edit**. Click on it, and a **pop-up window** opens.

This window is like a mini ticket interface: it shows ticket fields and the comment section. Update any system or custom field on the left-hand side. Leave a public or private comment in the middle section. Macros are available too. And, as with single tickets, you need to save your changes to the tickets by selecting an appropriate Status and then clicking Submit. After you click Submit, the window disappears, and Zendesk updates the tickets.

Don't get too trigger happy

For a batch of tickets, you have the same privileges as for individual tickets. But be careful, with great power comes great responsibility:

- You can choose to **merge** multiple tickets into one, but this can't be undone.
- You can **Delete** all the selected tickets (if you have the privileges), but only an Administrator has the ability to recover them.
- You can also mark a batch of tickets as **spam** (if you have the user rights), which moves the tickets into the View for spam and suspends the users. Unfortunately, both actions are time-consuming to remedy.

So, look twice at what option you choose when updating tickets in bulk.

Limitations

There are some limitations to bulk updating tickets, though. You can select more than 30 tickets at once, but the upper limit is a total of 100 tickets in one go. So if you want to update more than 100 tickets, you need to update them in batches of 100 and then repeat the process for the subsequent batches.

Also, it's worth mentioning that you can't update Closed tickets, which means that you can't select them in Views. Zendesk prevents any changes to them, as single tickets or in bulk.

Even though it appears that you can change every ticket field in the bulk update window, some cannot be changed. For example, Requester, CC, and Followers are a few of the fields not available in the bulk ticket update.

When to use it

You will come across some reasons to change several tickets in one go when working in Zendesk.

Maybe you just worked your way through 15 tickets and forgot to add a Tag or update a ticket field. Go back to your recent tickets and then select and update them all at once.

Or, if another Agent is not working today (planned or unplanned), you can go to their user profile, select all tickets currently assigned to them, and then distribute them amongst the team.

Did your team just get a bunch of similar requests from different Requesters? Maybe due to a fault on a website or system? No problem. Find those tickets and update them in one go (and then create a Macro for any new incoming ticket with the same issue).

Tip: String several Zendesk functionalities together. For example, maybe an update to the system outage came in, and you want to update the tickets related to that outage. Search for those tickets, select them all, and then apply a comment or Macro to update all of them in bulk.

Highlights

Select and edit up to 100 tickets in one go. You can do this from almost any ticket list in Zendesk (anywhere the checkboxes are available). Change almost everything you can on individual tickets and even apply Macros—but double-check before submitting updates! Correcting a mistake on that scale can be time-consuming.

Next, we'll work through two examples to showcase what I just described.

Follow along — Search and bulk update (5 minutes)

Ideally, you have some **test tickets** that are not Solved yet. If you don't have any, please **create a handful** now and assign them to yourself. Now log in as an Agent in your trial account.

Send updates to all waiting Customers
1) Go to **All unsolved tickets**.
2) **Select the first ticket** in the first row by clicking on the **checkbox** at the left of the Ticket Status.

3) Repeat this until you have **selected two or more tickets**. Then, Zendesk shows a checkmark on the left and highlights the selected rows in a different colour.

4) Click on **Edit x tickets** in the top right in the View. The x stands for the number of tickets you have currently selected. So, if you choose 3 tickets it will say **Edit 3 tickets**. This button only appears once you start selecting tickets.

5) In the new window that opens, go to the **Tags** field on the left. Enter **bulk_update,** and then a comma, a tab, or press Enter to confirm.

6) Then **go to the Macro drop-down** and select the Macro **Downgrade and inform**. Notice how the **Priority is set to Low,** and a **public comment** is added.

7) Next, **click the Submit** button.

8) Zendesk displays a little message and **update the tickets in the background**. Another message will confirm when your update is complete.

Tip: There is a drop-down to pick a Status for all those tickets. If you submit and choose Open, Zendesk will update all tickets with that Status. If you click the Submit button without selecting a Status, Zendesk will update all tickets without changing the Status. The system will apply all the other changes you made, but each ticket's Status remains as is. So, open tickets stay Open and Pending tickets stay Pending, etc. Search and update tickets in bulk

1) Go to the **search box** in the navbar, enter **updated>1month**, and press enter.

2) A new tab opens, and the results page will **show all tickets updated within the last month.**

3) Open the **filters drop-down** on the top right and add the following under Tags: **bulk_update.** If you can't select the Tag bulk_update in the filter, you need to **refresh the browser.**

4) As soon as Zendesk recognises the Tag, it updates the results page. It **shows only tickets with that Tag.**

5) **Select all tickets** by ticking the checkbox above all the tickets in the list.

6) Click **Edit x tickets.** The x stands for the number of tickets you have currently selected.

7) In the new window, click **Internal note.**

8) Enter the text:

   Customers were informed about the delay.

9) Click **Submit as Open.**

10) Zendesk **updates the tickets in the background** and will inform you about the progress.

Using shortcuts in Zendesk

When I started working with computers, we needed to install software the old way: using a data carrier such as a CD-ROM and then running the installation routine. You installed it on your local hard drive, restarted your computer, and got yourself a cup of coffee while the computer was busy. Then, you would pray to the computer gods that everything would work as expected and that your new software would run correctly.

The interface of this software would allow you to do exciting things. For example, you could enter data and browse existing information. But, usually, these applications were not pretty or easy to use. Actually, most of them were ugly. Fun fact— Zendesk was founded partly because of those old fashioned systems. The founders thought that CS software was cumbersome to use and felt user-unfriendly.

However, there was one advantage to this kind of software. Once mastered, proficient users could browse through the program at an unimaginable speed. People would gather around those "computer adepts" in awe. Screens would show up and disappear faster than you thought possible. The cursor would jump across the monitor to different fields until the user found the right one. Then, a couple of keystrokes later, the data was filled in, the window closed, and the next screen would appear. All this while the other input devices were seemingly left untouched.

Was this a hacker doing his magic? Was this a computer adept moving the mouse cursor with his mind? Were his hands too fast to see that he touched the mouse? Does he have a touchpad under his desk that he moves with his toes?

No, my friends. The answer is simple: keyboard shortcuts.

Those programs have been developed by engineers with efficiency in mind, not necessarily the ease of use. As a result, user-friendliness was not much of a concern most of the time. Before touchscreens, touchpads, or even computer mice, there was only one way of manipulating stuff on the monitor, through the computer keyboard. This means everything was doable by using the arrow and tab keys to move across the screen. When this is your only way of navigating the software, using a shortcut was a great way of saving time and effort.

And this, my friends, is the story of how keyboard shortcuts came to be–at least that's what I imagine.

Why this intro with a history lesson, you ask? I wanted to make a point.

Most software applications nowadays are simple-to-use, not complex. They often act as a front-end to a cloud service. For some, no app is needed; the service simply runs in a browser—like Zendesk. But Zendesk has been designed "properly". The good old values of those early computer engineers lived on. The developers made shortcuts available to us, despite running in a browser.

Interested? Excited? You should be! Let's dig in.

What are keyboard shortcuts

Shortcuts are a way to send one or more commands using the keyboard to the system. This way, you might not need a pointing device like a touchpad or computer mouse to do something. They often require pressing keys in a specific sequence and holding several keys down simultaneously. It can feel a bit like yoga for your fingers.

Why bother

If the whole intro wasn't enough to convince you, then maybe you will get more excited when I mention buzzwords such as "productivity hack" and "timesaver".

When working through a lot of tickets, you likely want to move fast. That's where shortcuts come in handy. They allow you to apply changes to tickets and move through the user interface without using the mouse or touchpad. In other words, if your hands are on the keyboard, you can quickly move through tickets without leaving that position.

By default, the shortcuts are activated for you as an Agent, and you can use them straight away in your browser when in Zendesk. Just press the right combination of keys, and Zendesk complies.

Keyboard shortcuts help in various ways

With shortcuts, you can do the following:

- Move quickly around the user interface
- Jump within and between tickets
- Update tickets with comments and apply Macros

One quick example:

1) [**ctrl**] + [**alt**] +[**v**] pressed at the same time opens the Views in Zendesk.

2) Use the **cursor** or **arrow** keys to select any ticket.

3) Press [**enter**] or [**return**] on your keyboard.

4) On the ticket windows, press [**ctrl**] +[**alt**] +[**m**] to open the Macro box.

5) Select a Macro with the up or down **arrow** keys and press [**enter**] or [**return**].

6) Press [**ctrl**] +[**alt**] +[**s**] at the same time to submit the ticket as Solved.

These keyboard shortcuts work in your browser; this is the case for Mac (macOS), Windows, and Linux machines. For macOS, you need to replace the [alt] key with the [option] key, but this should be easy to learn since they are next to each other on a typical Mac keyboard.

Complete list of shortcuts

I prepared a handy overview of shortcuts for Zendesk. You can <u>download them as PDF from my website</u>[23].

Tip: Download and learn some of these shortcuts. Print the PDF and put it next to your monitor for the first week or so. There is also a website[24] where you can practice them in a sort of mini-game. If you run the practice or test, it will ask you to press the correct keys for a specific action. It could be a fun way of internalising them.

What shortcuts to use

Here are the two sets of shortcuts every Agent should know and use. Even if you don't usually use shortcuts, I would recommend that you learn and use at least these two kinds of shortcut:

- Apply Macro
- Submit ticket (with a Status)

---

[23] <u>www.nilsrebehn.com/books-zendesk-for-agents-downloads</u>
[24] See bibliography on page 246

Apply Macro

You know how valuable Macros are because they can apply several changes in one go. They are even more powerful if you can use them *on the go* with only your keyboard.

1) Press [ctrl] + [alt] + [m] together to bring up the Macro list.
2) Start typing the name of a Macro and select it with the up or **down arrow** keys.
3) Press [enter] or [return] to apply it.

Submit ticket

For every Ticket Status in Zendesk, there is a shortcut you can use. The most useful ones for your everyday life as an Agent are the following. Apply either of them to a ticket you are working on.

1) [ctrl] +[alt] +[p] to submit a ticket as Pending.
2) [ctrl] +[alt] +[s] to submit a ticket as Solved.

Then, string shortcuts together: open a ticket from a View, review it, apply a suitable Macro, submit with the relevant Status and move to the next one. Repeat till the View is empty.

What could possibly go wrong?

In some circumstances, shortcuts might not work at all or not as expected. This might happen because other shortcuts are already in place, for example, from your operating system. Or, you have set up manual shortcuts that collide with the ones supported by Zendesk.

You can go into the computer settings and deal with it. Deactivate the shortcuts that collide or replace them with something that doesn't interfere. Or, if you want to keep your system or custom shortcuts, you can deactivate the shortcuts in Zendesk altogether.

I'm such a big fan of this way of working that I would keep them active and deal with the collisions–at least for the most valuable shortcuts. But if you still want to deactivate them, you can do the following:

1) Click on your **profile** icon in the top bar of Zendesk.
2) Select **Keyboard shortcuts** from the list.
3) Find the checkbox **Enable keyboard shortcuts** and remove the checkmark if it's there.
4) Click **Close** or anywhere outside the window to save the changes.

Wrap up

I love shortcuts, and you could too! Try them out. Learn the most important ones. Be a bit geeky. Save time.

Extending Zendesk via Apps

Zendesk comes with a lot of functionality and features out of the box. Admins can create complex workflows with the available features. They can tailor the system for very different scenarios and processes. That's why it's such an excellent fit for thousands of companies across various industries, from very small to very large teams.

There are plenty of similarities amongst businesses. How they operate their Customer Service and how they support their Customers. However, no two companies are alike. Every team works differently. Requirements of companies or how teams need to operate differ. Maybe they have some unique processes for their Customers, or they have complex demands for the data they collect and process. Perhaps they have systems that need to interact with tickets in Zendesk somehow.

And that is where Zendesk apps come in. These applications can add the functionality needed or connect to an external system. As a result, they can close the gap for companies and turn Zendesk into a 100% tailor-fit solution.

I always compare apps in Zendesk to how it works on smartphones. Your phone comes with a lot of fundamental functionality, but you can install an app that allows you to do things that are not built-in. Or, they will enable you to connect to a third party from your phone.

Zendesk apps, like on a smartphone, can be added via a dedicated marketplace. Administrators install and manage them, but most of them will be used by Agents. That's why we will cover different kinds of apps and how to use them.

Apps in Zendesk

Your Zendesk trial does not come with any apps, so you won't find any if you look for them. But, if apps are installed, they can be found in one of four different places:

1) The **navbar** on the left. Apps will install a new icon, and they will appear below the system icons.

2) The **top bar**. Icons for apps would typically appear to the left of system icons.

3) **Profiles** of Organisations and users. If installed, they would show up on the right-hand side of an Organisational or user profile.

4) **Tickets**. On the right-hand side is a special panel for apps, usually referred to as the apps tray. Other apps are placed in the comment section, next to the formatting options.

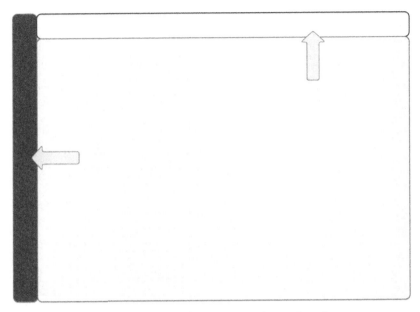
Figure: Possible app locations, navbar and top bar.

The app developer defines where the app will show up and how the icon looks, not the Admin. There are a few apps that are available in a few different places.

Tip: Some apps are not visible to Agents or don't have any user interface at all, like the Slack app. They still need to be installed and configured by an Admin, though.

Again, you won't see any apps in your trial account. Therefore, the navbar and top bar will only show the system icons. On the Organisation or user profile, you will see an empty apps tray. Same for the ticket window.

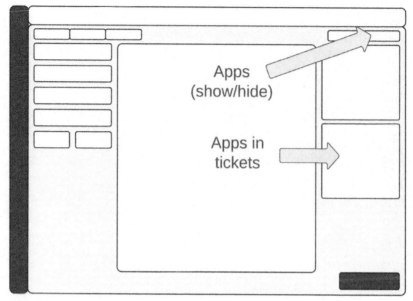

Figure: Apps in the apps tray on tickets. Show or hide them with the button.

If you are on a profile or ticket and don't see the apps tray, you can show (and hide it) by clicking the Apps button at the top.

The three types of apps

The location is one way to differentiate apps in Zendesk, but I would categorise apps in Zendesk in these main categories because most apps will do one of the following:

A. **Add functionality** that's not native to Zendesk or make an existing feature easier to use.

B. **Connect** to another system **to display** information within Zendesk.

C. **Connect** to another system **to read and write** information from the other System into Zendesk or vice versa or both.

Type B and C apps are often referred to as integrations (because they integrate parts of an external system into Zendesk). But, I want to point out the difference between them: type B integrations pull (read) the data to show extra details to the Agent. In contrast, type C integrations can show (read) external information and send it back (write).

In theory, any type of app can reside in any location within the Zendesk UI. So you can have an app of type A in user profiles, ticket pages and in the navbar, for example.

The app developer sets the location depending on where the Agent or Admin needs to access it. The purpose influences the location.

Tip: The most commonly used apps in a live Zendesk are apps on tickets accessed via the apps tray on the right-hand side of tickets.

Examples of apps by type

Type A

Apps of this type are often simple apps *to do something*. For example, they can show more information from within Zendesk or allow changing something within Zendesk. Examples are:

- **User Data** shows details from the user profile within the ticket. This can save you time because you don't need to click on the user profile to view information stored there.

- **Download All Attachments** does what it promises. It allows you to download all (and individual) attachments with one click. Very handy if Requesters submitted loads of images or PDFs in one ticket. Save time scrolling through the ticket history and access them in one place.

- **Tasks and Subtickets** add checklists and mini-project management capability to Zendesk. First, add lists of tasks to tickets. Convert jobs to sub-tickets. This allows you to split off several tickets from one main ticket. Agents can then work on them separately.

- **Knowledge Capture** allows you to search the help centre of your Zendesk (if there is content). You can then insert links to the articles into the ticket. The app also allows you to add content to the help centre from within tickets. This is a great way to utilise existing articles or build them up.

Type B

Apps in this category display information within Zendesk. They are often referred to as integrations. Here are a few examples:

- **Shopify** connects Zendesk to the e-commerce platform of the same name. It brings order information into the ticket. This way, you can help the End User without asking the Customer for order details or leaving Zendesk and searching the other system.

- **Shipup** is an app to display shipping information from over 70 shipping carriers. Access details on deliveries via DHL, FedEx, UPS or others from within the ticket. Again, no need to ask for more information as the app will query the carrier's platform. It then shows the available information next to the ticket.

- **Zoho CRM** integrates with the Zoho CRM, which stores Customer details such as contact information and more. The app pulls the Requester's information from the CRM platform and displays it right next to the ticket. No need to go search for the user in another window.

All apps of type B are one-way integrations. This means that Zendesk does not write data back into another system, which brings us to the following type of apps.

<u>Type C</u>

These apps are probably the most complex type. They connect to a third party system to bring information into Zendesk and then write it back. They are two-way integrations. Examples are:

- **Salesforce** connects Zendesk to Salesforce. In its simplest form, the app displays information from Salesforce in the ticket. Most CRM integrations work like this. But, this specific integration can also synchronise user and ticket data between the systems.
- **Trello** is an app to connect your projects and tasks from Trello to tickets in Zendesk. You can link tickets to existing boards and cards in Trello or create new ones from within a Zendesk ticket.
- **Slack** connects Zendesk to the collaboration tool. For example, you can send notifications from tickets to channels on Slack. You can also create tickets with comments from Slack in Zendesk. Fun fact: this app does not have an icon, buttons, or user interface in Zendesk. It's only accessible via Slack.

All apps on this list are available at the time of this writing. Unfortunately, I can't promise the availability of them after the release of the book. Still, the examples give you an idea of what kind of applications are available and the purpose they can serve.

Tip: Don't worry too much about the type of app and where it's installed. This overview just demonstrates what kind of apps you might come across.

If you start working on a live Zendesk, your manager will instruct you about what apps to use in your work. That's typically part of the onboarding process.

Solving tickets on the go

With your laptop and Zendesk in your web browser, you're pretty mobile and ready to solve tickets on the go. Yet, there might be times where you are out and about *without* your computer and still need to access tickets.

For this, Zendesk provides apps for your smartphone or tablet. These are not like the apps you install in your Zendesk from our previous chapter. Here we'll cover the mobile apps you can install on your smartphone or tablet to access Zendesk–not the apps you install in your Zendesk instance and access via the browser.

The mobile app functionality

The following is not a complete list but is instead a quick summary of what you can do with the Zendesk app for mobile devices:

- View existing or create new tickets.
- Update system and custom ticket fields.
- Add public or internal comments.
- Apply Macros.
- Assign to Agents, Groups, or add Followers and CCs.
- Mark tickets as spam or delete them.

Tip: You still need to submit a ticket when making changes on a ticket via the mobile app. This is like working in the browser. Updates are only saved (and comments sent to users) when you submit the ticket.

User interface

Tickets page

This page is comparable to the Views panel in the browser version: select a View to see all tickets. It's the same list you would see in the desktop version. It provides access for up to 12 global and 8 personal Views.

You can access a single ticket by tapping on it. In addition, you can bulk update tickets by tapping **edit** and then selecting several tickets. You can then update fields and comments. You can also merge them, mark them as spam, or delete the chosen tickets altogether.

Search page

This is similar to what we covered before: search for anything in users or tickets. However, you won't be able to access Organisations. Also, filter options are limited.

Notifications page

This page shows you any notifications from the last 30 days. The latest notifications are displayed first, and the older ones below. You can update the list by swiping down.

You can tap any notification to open the respective ticket. It will then be marked as read. Of course, you can mark all notifications as read if you don't want to open all of them individually.

<u>Settings page</u>

You can change anything related to the app and notifications here. However, you can't access your Zendesk settings, such as editing personal Views or Macros from the mobile app.

When to use it

Whenever I am travelling, I use the app on my phone to check on tickets. The app allows me to leave my computer at home and still review, update, and assign tickets.

You can search, sort, and filter tickets in Views. You can also create new tickets and comment or update existing ones. Notifications will tell you if there is something you need to look at.

Some companies work across different countries and time zones. That means teams might need to cover late evenings, early mornings, or even weekends. If you don't need to work on and solve tickets, the mobile apps might be just what you need. Check on Views regularly, update tickets where necessary, and escalate to people when needed.

The mobile app might be enough if you need to *keep an eye on* something after hours, if you are on standby duty to monitor Customer Support, if you are just triaging incoming tickets, or when taking an extended lunch break.

It's not powerful enough to replace the desktop version of Zendesk, but it bridges the gap for use in-between.

What to not use it for

Next, let's talk about the limitations of the mobile apps for Zendesk Support:

- A smaller screen–obviously. You can see fewer details of a ticket and, unless you have a hardware keyboard hooked to your mobile device, typing with your fingers will probably be much slower.
- You can only work on asynchronous tickets, those that came in via email or web widget.
- No access to Zendesk apps in the mobile app. The apps I described previously, such as Shopify and Salesforce, can't be accessed from within the mobile apps. They run only on the browser version of Zendesk.

Notifications

Notifications from the mobile app can inform you of any changes that happened to tickets. For example, when turned on, the app can notify you of all New tickets, tickets in your Groups, or when you are an Assignee, CC, or Follower. You can also turn them completely off to receive none.

If you turn notifications on, you can specify the hours and days you want to receive them. These notifications can be push notifications to your smartphone display, simple indicators on your app icon, only notifications within the app—or a combination of those.

I have a firm opinion about notifications in general. With our modern lifestyle, there is a tendency to receive too many of them—not only from work but also in our personal life. I think we need to be in control of our time and focus. Therefore, in my opinion, you should manage what notifications to receive and when.

I could write a whole chapter on notifications and distractions from devices, but I just want to give you the advice to think about the following in the context of Zendesk:

- Where do/will you work in Zendesk mostly—desktop or mobile?
- What kind of notifications would you need from the mobile app—and when?
- Is it enough to have no notifications and use the mobile app on demand?
- Do you need to be alerted about updates?

I personally turned the notifications on for tickets assigned to me or where I'm a CC or Follower. Then, I limited it to my office hours during weekdays. That works for me because I'm usually the escalation point in my company.

Configure your setup accordingly.

Summary

The mobile app is not a power tool for working on a lot of tickets. That's due to the limitations of the screen size and some missing functionality. Yet, in specific scenarios, it can still be super handy to check, distribute, or escalate tickets.

A Day In The Life Of An Agent

This section is about how Zendesk can be used in real life. You'll see the journey of agents throughout their workday. I hope to show you how everything you learned is coming together.

However, the names, characters, business, events, and incidents are the products of my imagination (except for references to Zendesk products and features). Any resemblance to actual persons, living or dead, or actual events is purely coincidental.

Chapter 1

The alarm goes off and causes Tom's ears to ring. He reaches out into the darkness, not knowing what he will find. But he has to; the situation is dire, and the alarm makes it hard to concentrate. Finally, his hand finds the device he's looking for.

Tom hits the button on his mobile phone to turn off the morning alarm. He hates the noise, but he puts up with it because it wakes him right up. He sits up and stretches. The sun is already up. But his curtains are blocking out most of the light, making it easier for him to sleep properly.

He makes his way to the bathroom, walking past a small tower of books. For the last couple of months, he's been studying lots of technical and systems stuff. More than his current job requires. Reading books helps him to reduce the ample screen time he racks up because of his career. But he mixes in online classes sometimes to make things more interesting.

"If I want to improve my situation, I need to do this", is what he once told his Dad on a video call. Tom has a good relationship with his parents. A few years back, when their business was struggling, he lent them some money. He couldn't help much since he doesn't have any experience in building or selling houses. And his savings were limited, but at least they were able to pay off their overdue tax and overcome the difficulties. Tom wishes he could have contributed more.

But for now, it's back to business. It's a lovely Monday morning. Or, at least he assumes that. It looks nice outside, but he has the early shift for this week and needs to get going. He fires up his computer. It's a laptop the company provided; a decent machine. Still, his workplace at home is not really what one would call a "home office". With the onset of the pandemic, the company asked everyone in the team to work from home. Technically possible, since almost everything can be done online anyway. But, when renting his one-bedroom apartment, he hadn't foreseen that it would be his workplace as well.

The big room holds his kitchen on one side and the lounge / living space on the other half. There is a good-sized table that serves as a dining table, study desk and work desk. For now, he cleans up the contents from last night; some books and an empty mug. He replaces it with a new cup, holding his fresh and steaming favourite morning beverage. The laptop is more than ready. He logs onto Zendesk and starts to work.

He works for the Customer Support team of a tech company. His team is regarded as the forefront of inbound communication. Internally it's referred to as Level 1 Support. Questions here are easy in comparison to Level 2, where they handle more technical queries. Tom hopes his efforts will be noticed and that his self-education will allow him to rise to the Level 2 team soon. Customer queries will be more advanced and less transactional than in his current role.

But for now, he enjoys the variety of questions and being able to help most of the customers by himself. With the early shift comes the duty of triaging. He's the first one looking through the pile of tickets that came in after office hours.

They have been using Zendesk for a while now. It made a lot of things more efficient: the majority of tickets are routed to the teams based on specific criteria. What's left for his team are the less complicated customer queries—and anything that the system could not assign automatically.

Tom enters the view for new tickets. After weekends, the count for tickets is high—as expected. He moves through them efficiently: assigning tickets to himself and other Groups. Later, he and his team will work on them.

There is one ticket that seems a bit odd. It looks like a reply to a previous message. Tom inspects the requester's profile and notices a pending ticket with another agent: Mary.

Tom looks up from his laptop and into the distance. From where he sits, he can look through the open curtains of his living room window. But, in front of his inner eye is the picture of Mary. She joined a few weeks back. He's never seen her in person due to the current restrictions. But he imagines how it would be to meet her. *Perhaps they could go out together and share a drink or a meal?*

He blinks a few times and comes back to reality. Tom looks at the screen and wonders what to do. "Maybe I can..." he thinks out loud. Then he starts typing.

Tom leaves an internal comment for her that only she can see. He explains that he saw this ticket and thinks it's related to the conversation she already had with the customer. But, rather than merging the tickets without context, he wanted to give her a choice. Then he adds an emoji and assigns the open ticket to her. She'll see it later in her queue when she comes online.

A few moments after submitting the update, Tom thinks about that ticket again: *Should I have just merged it for her? Will she think I'm lazy? And what about that stupid emoji. Man, I should have left it as is.*

But Tom's thoughts are interrupted by a popup: the team meeting. Right now.

Hang on, let's pause here for a minute.

What did you see so far in the life of Agent Tom?

- These days you can expect work from home arrangements.
- The company uses Zendesk as their Customer Service platform and routes tickets to teams based on specific rules.
- Tom uses Views to access tickets.
- The team seems to be on alternating shifts.
- Tom's shift entails triage, a process to screen and distribute tickets.
- He assigns a ticket to Mary with an internal comment for context.
- Tom likes Mary.

What happens next?

Chapter 2

He looks down. He's wearing something. Good. But it's still his sleepwear–not good!

Tom rushes to his bedroom to throw on a shirt. He checks himself in the mirror and combs his hair in a hurry. It looks okay now. That should suffice to look like a human being.

He stumbles back to the computer, brings up the meeting software, fumbles with his headset, and turns on the camera. "...birthday to you", blares out of his in-ear speakers. He's confused for a moment. Everyone sings–except for him and Matthew, his manager. *It's not my birthday, so it must be his,* Tom thinks in his confusion. He is quick to join the singing, hoping that no one notices.

"...to Matthew." Everyone applauds. He tries to find out if anyone realises that he joined a minute late. Tom checks the video feeds of his teammates. Everyone is accounted for. James, the guy who is senior to him and thinks he knows it all. Patricia, the chatty do-gooder who's always happy to help. Lawrence, a quiet guy who's very nice and always delivers on his promises. Matthew, older than everybody and trying to be a friend and manager to everyone. And there, in the corner of the screen, Mary. She is smiling, like most of the time. Her hair falls open over her shoulders.

Where did she get that silly birthday hat? Tom wonders. Now it's gone. She must have been using a filter or special effect to make it look like she's wearing a hat. She's smirking at her screen; *it seems like she's looking at someone in the team. But who? James, Lawrence, me?* No one can tell where someone is looking with this software; everyone's monitor displays people in a different order.

Tom catches himself staring at his screen while everyone breaks into chatter: "What is the big plan today, Matt?" asks James.

"You know, the usual: attending management meetings, lunch with my wife at home..." says Matt.

Patricia interrupts: "Anything else? Something you don't do every day?"

Matt stares away from the camera, then shrugs his shoulders: "Maybe getting a dessert?" People chuckle.

"Okay, nice. But no celebration?" probes Patricia again. "How about dinner with the team?" she asks.

Everyone has a big grin on their face now, and Matthew's mouth opens, but no words come out. *Is that today?* Tom thinks to himself. He remembers seeing an internal message and an invite from Patricia, who wanted to organise something nice for Matt and the team. Yes, the calendar app confirms: today is that day. Also, he had accepted the invite.

Patricia explains that Matt's wife is involved; she will drop him off and pick him up afterwards. The kids are taken care of. And yes, given the circumstances, everyone will be careful.

It will be the first outing for Tom in a while. The first time the team will meet in person for a long time. It's the first opportunity to meet Mary in real life.

The rest of the meeting is uneventful. The team's daily meeting is a place to discuss customer tickets and concerns. It lasts between 10 to 20 minutes on average. They talk about some edge cases where Level 2 might need to take a look. Also, Matt shares that their KPI for last month looks good, and encourages everyone to keep up the good work.

Then, towards the end, the meeting is almost over; people talk about what they will wear. Everyone agrees that long sleeves and protective gear are a good idea. But then James comments on Mary's top.

Hang on, was that a compliment? Does James fancy her? Does she like him? Does she know he's married? Why would he make such a comment? Tom is annoyed.

The meeting ends, and he closes his laptop. Tom walks over to the window, leans against the frame and stares outside. He doesn't notice cars and people passing by. Tom has been alone for a while now. The whole situation makes it hard to go out and meet people. Not that he's the outgoing type anyway. Tom likes the outdoors, but he's never been a big extrovert. He's okay with a small but intimate circle of people. Quality over quantity, he often says.

However, being by yourself, far away from family and without someone to love, can be challenging. Tom hopes moving to a different team will help him improve his finances, but also expose him to more people. Then, when Mary joined, he felt excited. He's happy to see her in meetings, even working together on tickets and messaging internally about work stuff.

But then James seems to make a move. That could really ruin things. Such a... then his thoughts trail off, and he goes back to work. The rest of the morning, he works through tickets. The one he assigned to himself earlier is quickly taken care of: select several of them and apply a suitable Macro. Done. He moves to the reopened tickets and reads through the customer comments. For the next few hours, he's absorbed by the flow. Then, towards noon, a message pops up on Slack, their internal communication tool. Tom checks Slack three times a day: mornings, after lunch, and before finishing his workday. But, he set it up in a way that personal messages, something addressed to him in private, pop up at any time. This way he won't miss important things.

And this could be important: it's a message from Mary.

Ok, let's take a break here.

What else did you see Agent Tom do today?

- Tom attends a daily meeting. Many teams in Customer Service use meetings like this to coordinate things and align on work to be done.
- Matthew mentions KPI (key performance indicators). These are numbers that management looks out for to understand how a team is performing.
- Tom uses Zendesk to update several tickets in one go. He seems to have experience with that kind of ticket.
- The company has set up different workflows for different kinds of tickets executed by Macros.
- The team uses Slack for internal communications. Platforms like this allow remote teams to collaborate.
- Tom is annoyed by James.

Now, what's this message about?

Chapter 3

Tom stops in his tracks. He switches apps and looks for the message from Mary. There are a handful of notifications for him, updates and such. They can wait. He's looking for something else. There, the message from Mary. One to one. Not in the group chat.

He smiles involuntarily and reads the message: "Hi Tom, sorry to interrupt you. Could you do me a favour, please? I promised Patricia to bring candles for the cake that she ordered. I wanted to do that on my lunch break, but something important came up. Can you please get some candles for the cake she ordered? And a lighter! Pleeease say yes. You're my only hope."

Tom rereads the lines. She used several emojis. This means his earlier message with the emoji should be acceptable. He just noticed that his heart is beating faster and that he's smiling.

She reached out directly to me to ask me for a favour. She must think I'm reliable. Or did she ask Lawrence first? He would definitely have said yes. Maybe someone else? And I'm the fallback? And what about the last sentence? Was that a Star Wars reference? Or pure coincidence?

Then he contemplates how to respond. He can think of some places where to get those items. *Maybe I can get them during my lunch break? I should say yes. But what do I send back? I don't want to seem too eager. It should look casual.*

Tom drafts a few replies until he has something that seems casual and not too eager. He hits send and waits for a response before he realises she's offline. That makes him a bit sad. After a short while, he shakes off the feeling and gets ready to go out. With proper trousers, appropriate shoes and a jacket, he leaves his apartment. It's warm enough outside, but a fresh breeze sweeps through the streets.

A few shops later, he's walking back home with his lunch and the requested items. Finding a lighter was easy enough, but candles for a birthday cake not so much. In the end, he got a pack of five small ones. And they are pink. It was the only option. Also, he forgot to ask how many they need. He doesn't even know how old his manager is as of today. *Guys don't talk about it much. It's gonna be okay,* he tells himself.

A little while later, in his apartment, Tom clears the table again. The book he was reading goes back to the pile, and the utensils he used for his lunch go to the kitchen. He wipes the table, starts up the laptop and logs back in again. Via Slack, he tells Mary he got the goods. Next, he's checking for open tickets assigned to him.

Indeed, a few of his previously solved tickets have been reopened. One Customer thanks Tom for his help, and another one has a follow-up question. Easy. But the third one is less easy. Actually, it's unpleasant: he remembers explaining to her how the refund procedure works. *Pretty straight forward* in Tom's opinion. But the requester came back

224

saying it doesn't work as described. And the message is not very polite.

Last week Tom double-checked that the refund form works as expected, asked the customer to try again and gave some tips on what to look out for. But apparently, it didn't work for her—or she didn't even try. And now the person came back complaining. The requester is flagged as VIP, which means Zendesk sets the tickets to priority high by default. That by itself doesn't stress Tom too much. He is really responsive and helps everyone equally well; at least that's what he'd like to think.

Yet, the more people that give him a favourable rating on the satisfaction survey, the better for him. And he certainly wants as few complaints as possible. A certain percentage is standard, and management expects that not every customer will be happy in the end. But with his ambition of moving to the other team, he can use all the help he can get. And the fewer complaints, the better.

After reading the message twice and checking again that the form works, he takes a deep breath and starts typing. He knows how frustrating it can be to be stuck with something so he puts himself into the position of the user and contemplates his reply. A few minutes later, he finished typing a comment for the requester, suggesting one other thing to try on her end. *It has to be on her side*, Tom thinks. He submits the ticket as solved.

By that time, Tom receives a reply from Mary. She thanks him for his help and is looking forward to tonight. The rest of the afternoon, he's spent working on new tickets for Level 1. He is on the lookout for reopened individual tickets. But he's really looking forward to tonight as well.

Working hours are over. He checks one last time: all new tickets are taken care of, and no open tickets for him. Perfect. Tom decides to freshen up in the bathroom and gets a set of clothes from his closet. He's not used to going out anymore; it has been a while. Also, he wants to look cool but approachable, fashionable but not like a hipster. Tom looks at his clothes and scratches his head.

A bit later, he's waiting outside for the ride he hailed via an app. It arrives, and he looks inside: it smells fresh and seems clean. Tom climbs into the backseat, and the driver takes off. *The driver doesn't like small talk and just plays music–good.* He uses the time to pull out his smartphone. He wonders where the others are and checks Slack and work emails. Tom would like to arrive early enough so he can choose where to sit.

That's when he sees an email notification: the VIP customer replied.

Stop, let's rewind.

What happened during the rest of the day for our Agent, Tom?

- Tom checks tickets assigned to him and replies to Open tickets. It is a best practice to reply to tickets and give them to the Agent that responded.
- He double-checks if something works as expected before replying to a Customer. Checking a process or functionality for the Customer is a good idea.
- The company gives VIP status to specific Customers to ensure their tickets are treated with a higher Priority.
- Customer satisfaction seems to play a role in this team. This is a common way for a business to measure how the support team is doing.
- Tom checks in on the Group Views and works on tickets from there. The workflow for the team is based on a shared View where every Agent finds their subsequent work.
- Tom is looking forward to seeing everyone, especially Mary.

So, what is the notification about? And will he arrive in time?

Chapter 4

Tom instantly gets nervous when he sees the email. He knows it's not the end of the world; some customers get upset. They are human beings, and humans can be reasoned with. He opens the email and reads it. Apparently, his latest suggestion did not help the customer, and he tells Tom about it. On the one hand, nothing too bad. On the other hand, her problem still exists–and Tom does not know how to help her any further.

He replies to the email, telling the customer that he'll look into it and gets back to him within the next day. Then he looks outside the window of the car. Buildings are flying by. It's getting dark. Streetlights are coming on. They wait at a traffic light. A few pedestrians are crossing. It's not very busy, even for a Monday. *People go out less these days*, thinks Tom to himself. *Dang, I haven't been out in a while. Wonder if I still know how to talk to people. And how do I greet people, do I shake hands? Hugs are out of the question, for sure. Waving?* He smiles to himself at the thought.

Then the car stops in front of the restaurant. He checks the app: the ride has been paid for. He thanks the driver and exits the vehicle. Tom briefly looks around for familiar faces, sees no one around and enters the building. He greets the staff at the entrance and disinfects his hands. "I'm with a group. They booked a table for...", Tom says and thinks. Then he continues, "...six people in total, I believe." The person points towards the restaurant's far end and says: "Yes, they are at the back. Please go past the bar and turn right."

Tom smiles and nods, then follows the instructions. He has never been to this restaurant before. Someone else from the team recommended it. The designer indeed used a lot of wood to decorate the place. It has a warm and rustic flair to it. As he walks past the bar area, he notices the pots and pans hanging from the ceiling. They look used; maybe it's the former kitchen equipment? How quirky, he thinks. Tom decides that he likes it here.

The tables and seats are generously spaced out. Lots of tables for two people and some can seat four. When he reaches the far end, the restaurant opens up to a broader area. This must be the space where they host groups of people. But at the moment there are only a couple of empty four-seater tables and a large one in the middle. And that's where he sees his colleagues.

Matt sits at the head of the table at the far end. Lawrence sits to his left, followed by Patricia. On the other side, he sees Mary sitting between Matt and James. And there is an empty seat next to James, pretty much opposite Matt.

How come everyone is here before me? And why is James right next to Mary? Tom's mood goes down by two notches. That's what he wanted to avoid.

James sees Tom, waves and shouts: "Hey Tom, good timing. We're about to order food". Lawrence and Patricia sit with their back to Tom. They turn around, smile and wave. Matt and Mary were holding the food menu but now look up too. Matt raises his hand and says: "Hi, good to see you. Have a seat and help us to pick starters." Mary smiles, says hi, and waves with her left empty hand.

Tom waives back at the round, smiles and says hello. He sits down, and they start ordering food and drinks. They soon exchange the usual pleasantries and small talk. As the starters arrive, the topic shifts to how everyone is coping with the situation. Working from home has been the dream for so many when they used to work from the company office. But now, being forced to work from home is not easy for everyone.

James has a lot of things to share and talks quite a bit. Not unusual for him, and it's mostly funny. But because of that, Tom finds it difficult to speak to the others. And it makes it virtually impossible to talk to Mary on the other side of James. He's waiting for an opportunity to join the chatter when Matt stands up and walks towards the toilet.

On the way, he stops next to Tom and says: "Hey, the views are as tidy as always when you are on triage. Very good. Quick question, though, I noticed there's an open ticket from Teck Stop assigned to you. You're on top of it, right?"

Tom blinks twice. He's a bit surprised. Then he remembers and replies: "Yes, that one. I actually updated it on the way here. And tomorrow, I will sort it out."

"I know you got it," says Matt and is on his way to the toilets. The starters are devoured quickly, and the mains arrive soon after. Drinks are refilled, and the conversation flows nicely. Tom still didn't have a chance to say anything to Mary. He looks towards her as often as he can without looking suspicious. He likes how she looks today. Tom never saw her in real life, so he can't tell how she looks on other days. But he likes how she looks today.

At some point, she looks at him. The waitress removes the empty dishes from the main course. Mary gestures and points at him. It looks like she tries to turn on an invisible lighter. No one else notices due to the commotion. He understands and nods. She points behind him to the corridor. Mary gets up and excuses herself. Tom wonders how long he should wait. He decides this was a decent amount and gets up to it. James notices it and gives him a thumbs-up, and winks at him with his left eye.

What the heck? What does that mean? What do you think I'm doing? He takes the few steps towards the door with the sign for the restrooms and walks through. It's a long corridor with a few doors leading in different directions. At the far end, he sees the next sign for the restrooms. But to the left is an open door and a bright light shines into the corridor. Mary stands there with a big cardboard box in both hands. It seems to be the backdoor to the kitchen.

"Hey, the staff kept the cake in the fridge for us. How nice. Did you bring the candles and the lighter?" she asks with a smile.

He holds up the pack of five pink sticks of wax plus the lighter and says, "of course."

"Ok, let me put them on and light them up. Here, can you hold the cake?" Mary asks and turns the box towards him. It rests on her forearms with her hands securing the edge pointing at Tom. He brings the box between them, and his hands grab the underside on Mary's side. The weight of the cake rests on his forearms, and she slides back her arms. Her hands touch his hands briefly while she makes sure the box is secured. They smile at each other.

"How old is Matt today," asks James. They both look at James, who suddenly stands next to them. Mary shrugs and then says: "I don't know. You should know better." James is quiet and seems to think.

"However, how about this..." Mary says and rips away the packaging. "The cake has four corners. We put a candle towards each corner," she says while placing them in each corner.

"If he's in his forties, it's okay since there are four candles. If he's still in his thirties, it's okay too: since there is a candle in each of the four corners, they can't possibly represent his age."

Tom smiles and nods. He likes that logic. James nods as well. It seems like he can't think of a clever response. Mary grins from ear to ear and says: "Lighter, please, it's showtime!"

The three of them return to the table and start singing; the others join in. Now it's Matt that has a big grin across his face. They cheer and let glasses clink. He blows the candles and—as tradition wants it—doesn't share his wish. Tom wishes it would be his birthday today.

He certainly knows what to wish for.

Ok, hold my drink.

Our Agent Tom is off duty, but is there still something to note?

- Tom received an email notification for one of the tickets assigned to him. He replied to the email, which triggered a public response. This is a default setting in Zendesk and comes in handy if Agents are not at their desk but have access to their emails.
- Remote working comes with its challenges. Teams need to address them and find ways to make it work for everyone.
- Matt has specific Views to monitor certain parts of their Zendesk. This is standard practice for team leads and managers to make sure that tickets above Normal Priority or "old" tickets are taken care of.
- Tom likes Mary's sense of humour.

Will Tom have another chance to talk to Mary?

Chapter 5

If anyone had measured the mood at the table, they would have seen it climbing up over the evening. The peak certainly was the sharing of the cake. Everyone ate a slice or two. And everyone enjoyed being out with the team. Patricia documented the evening with a good amount of pictures. Over the following weeks, they would appear on Slack whenever the team needed to lift their spirits.

Matt asked over and over if anyone wanted another slice. But he did not find any more takers. Everyone was happy, and so he closed the lid of the box. His wife and kids will help him with the rest at home. Most glasses were empty, and no one ordered a refill. All good things must come to an end, so some people started leaving.

First, it was Matt's turn; his wife picked him up as promised. Then Lawrence and Patricia excused themselves. They are not a couple, but live in the same part of town, so they called a ride to share and left.

This leaves Tom, James, and Mary. James still sits between them. Tom regrets that he did not have any opportunity to talk to Mary. There was no logical excuse to change seats. And he couldn't think of any reason to get some privacy. *Why are you still here, James? Don't you need to go home too?*

At some point, he can't hold it back anymore. The pressure becomes too much. He stands up, looks at the two of them. And says: "Excuse me, got to use the restroom." Tom walks off to the toilets.

Dang, couldn't I have said something cooler? How can going to the restrooms be cool anyway? And this James... is he flirting with Mary. Does he like her? Tom continues his thoughts while being on autopilot.

He does not know how much time has passed when he returns. But as he steps back into the restaurant, he notices the table is empty. Everyone is gone—no James or Mary. Only the waitress is around, cleaning up a few leftovers. She smiles politely and walks away with both hands full.

Thoughts are running through his head: *How long was I away? Why did they not say goodbye? Did they leave together?*

He sits down in his chair. If the eating of the cake was the peak of the mood, the barometer suddenly hit rock bottom. His gaze wanders across the table. All glasses have been cleared. He wants to distract himself. Tom pulls out his phone and stares at the screen.

Then suddenly a voice behind him says: "You're still here. Good." He turns around and sees Mary coming from the corridor leading to the restrooms. He starts grinning as his mood instantly improves. Tom adjusts the grin to a friendly smile and expects Mary to walk past him to her chair. But she plops down right next to him, where Patricia sat before.

"Man, James can certainly talk a lot," she says and smiles. It's a big smile mixed with a chuckle. Tom likes the look of it. And the sound of it.

"Yes, he's fun to be around, though," he replies.

"Oh yeah, don't get me wrong. It's just that I thought it's already a lot during the online meetings. But in real life... even more."

Tom smiles and nods.

"Was I interrupting anything," she asks while pointing at his phone. Tom looks down at his hands, still holding the device. He hesitates, thinking of what to say. *She should not think I was texting anyone, like a girlfriend or so... Quick, say something.*

"Well, I was checking on this one ticket, " Tom hears himself saying. *Oh no*, he thinks to himself. *Now she thinks I can't switch off from work. Or that I'm a nerd who's striving for the best grades. How lame.*

"Oh really, why is it bothering you. Can I see it?"

He starts the Zendesk app and locates the ticket. Then he hands her his phone and says: "Here, it's from Teck Stop, our VIP customer. They want a refund. But for some reason, she has a problem initiating the refund. And I can't figure out how to help her."

"I see," she says while studying the comments. It was a bit of a back and forth but not too much. Tom looks at her from the side. *She looks even better than in the online meetings.*

She turns to him, smiles and says: "I think I know what you can do". Tom raises his eyebrows and looks surprised. "Here, let me show you." Mary leans towards him and holds up his smartphone and says: "Look, she's not getting anywhere, and we can't figure out the problem. She can't submit the documents through the form for some reason—but they are attached to the ticket already. If that happens, there is an alternative. There is a new escalation path for those incidents. It goes straight to finance, and they take care of the refund manually."

Then she taps a few buttons and explains: "There is a new Macro for this. Apply. Double check. Looks good. Submit.". Mary looks up and says, "There you go, it's on its way." She hands him his phone with a grin.

Tom looks at her, still surprised. He manages to say "thank you" and smiles. His hand reaches out to the phone. Their hands are touching. They smile at each other.

Ticket solved — The End.

So, what did you learn?

- The mobile app can be convenient when you need to review or update a ticket on the go.
- Workflows can change over time. They are usually improved or updated by managers or Administrators.
- Macros are your best friends for workflows. Teams should manage and update them regularly.
- Always read company updates so that you know the latest changes to workflows, policies, etc.
- Mary might like Tom too.

This wraps up the day in the life of an Agent.

What's Next

First, well done to you!

You just completed a non-fiction book and educated yourself on a topic that many people would consider to be a bit dry. However, helping customers and knowing the tools involved is very beneficial. And, since Zendesk is the market leader in this sector, it will come in handy.

Updates

Second, subscribe to get updates and errata on this book. I was as thorough as possible, but there might be some mistakes in this book that I need to correct later on. And, I plan to update this book when Zendesk introduces changes to the Agent experience.

Sign up for book updates at:

www.nilsrebehn.com/books-zendesk-for-agents-updates.

More resources

There are a few online resources mentioned throughout this book. Here is a list of all of them and how to access them.

Download all the resources to this book at

www.nilsrebehn.com/books-zendesk-for-agents-updates

All exercises

If you haven't already done so, you can do all the practical exercises now in one go. It should take you between 60 to 90 minutes.

Find the complete list of exercises in the table of contents[25].

---

[25] See Table Of Contents on page 11

Glossary

Here are the terms used in this book, with their definitions, in alphabetical order.

- **Administrator (Admin)** - In the IT context, it is a person who is responsible for the configuration and maintenance of a system. They usually have more **user** rights than other users in the system.

- **Agent** - A term often used to describe a Customer Service role. Job titles commonly used are "Customer Service Agent" or "Customer Support Representative". Their main job is to help customers with their questions and issues.

- **API** (Application Programming Interface) - Defines and allows interactions between multiple systems.

- **CS** - Can be short for one of the following. The terms are often used interchangeably and can mean different things to different people. In this book, we talk primarily about Customer Service.

  - **Customer Support**. It is mainly reactive and deals with specific customer questions and problems. Their work usually starts after the purchase of a product or service.

  - **Customer Service**. This part of the business takes care of customers' concerns. A good team engages with customers before, during, and after the sale. Customer Service can cover technical and non-technical issues.

- ○ **Customer Success**. This department works closely with other parts of the business and its customers. They touch on several aspects of the customer journey. A lot of companies emphasise post-sales engagements and tend to be proactive. Customer Success is often a different department that works together with Service or Support.

- **CRM** (Customer Relationship Management) - Describes the process of managing interactions with potential and existing customers. A CRM system helps companies manage customer relationships and run operations.

- **Help Centre** - Contains articles for Users to find answers to their support issues. In Zendesk, this is provided by Guide, which is used as a knowledge base for support articles and FAQs.

- **Omnichannel** - Describes a system or a strategy across different channels. Organisations use an omnichannel strategy to improve their user experience across their contact points. All communication channels and resources are designed for efficient integration onto the same omnichannel platform.

- **SaaS** (Software as a Service) - Software is accessed online rather than installed on computers, often licensed via a subscription rather than a one-time fee.

- **Ticket** - In Customer Service, it represents an object that stores details about an interaction with one or several users. It often represents questions, problems, and tasks that need to be worked on.

- **Ticket ID or Ticket Number** - This is the reference number related to a specific ticket.

- **Ticketing system** - It's a system that receives and manages questions and issues (see ticket). It allows teams to collaborate and work on these queries in an organised way, often employing processes.

- **Use Case** - Describes a situation in which a product or service could be used. For example, a typical use case for Zendesk is eCommerce and retail. A lot of companies in those sectors are using the platform.

- **Webform** - This is any form on a website that asks for details from the user.

- **Workflow** - A workflow describes a sequence of specific steps until completion. Workflows can be part of a bigger process. For example, it's common to have a workflow to process refunds in eCommerce or retail companies.

Bibliography

Here are the citations and links to all resources and documents referenced in the book, ordered by appearance.

What you'll need

- **Top 5 Benefits of a Hands-on Learning Approach** by EC Education, https://www.universities-colleges-schools.com/article/top-5-benefits-of-a-hands-on-learning-approach

- Recommended web browser, see **Zendesk Support system requirements** by Zendesk, https://support.zendesk.com/hc/en-us/articles/203661786-Zendesk-Support-system-requirements

- **Free Zendesk trial**, https://www.zendesk.com/register/ if for whatever reason that doesn't work, go to https://www.zendesk.com/ and look for a "free trial", "sign up" or "get started" button on the homepage.

What a ticket is

- **Ticket** (n.) by the Online Etymology Dictionary, https://www.etymonline.com/word/ticket

- **Issue tracking system**, see **ticket** by Wikipedia https://en.wikipedia.org/wiki/Issue_tracking_system

Where tickets come from

- **What Is an Acceptable Waiting Time?** by Call centre Helper, https://www.callcentrehelper.com/omnichannel-acceptable-waiting-time-140566.htm

Your role in Zendesk

- **Understanding Zendesk Support user roles** by Zendesk, https://support.zendesk.com/hc/en-us/articles/203661776-Understanding-Zendesk-Support-user-roles

Becoming an Agent

- **Best email services: paid, free and business providers** by Tech Radar Pro, https://www.techradar.com/news/best-email-provider

Zooming into ticket fields

- **About custom field types** by Zendesk, https://support.zendesk.com/hc/en-us/articles/203661866

Agent profile photo

- **A globally recognised Avatar** by Gravatar, http://en.gravatar.com/

Searching in Zendesk

- **Search...** by Zendesk, look for "search operators", https://support.zendesk.com/hc/en-us/articles/203663226#topic_ngr_frb_vc

Keyboard shortcuts

- **Practising shortcuts** by Ninja Dojo, https://www.shortcutfoo.com/app/dojos/zendesk

Acknowledgements
(Credits)

The last words in this book belong to the people that helped me throughout the process.

I want to thank **Meicel** for her support in all my ventures. Especially for her patience while listening to me going on and on about this book. Thank you.

A thank you goes to the editors and illustrators that helped in the process.

But I want to say a big thank you to all my friends that helped to make this book better, especially the following individuals (in alphabetical order):

Ingmar Zahorsky, who helped to make the exercises and examples more tangible.

Martin Lingel, who spotted that this book lacked the keen eye of a native speaker.

Michael Goh, who I thank for the fact that this book has screenshots.

Nicolas Goetz, who found stuff others overlooked.

Roberto Aiello, the designer and instructor, who gave good feedback.

Sofyan Afqir, the Zendesk expert who found some things I overlooked.

A very special thanks goes to the editor in chief. The man who stepped up when I couldn't find the right editor. A man of his word who would honour a promise down to the last sentence: **Anton de Young**, the editor who made this book so much better.

Thank you so much, everyone. I'm very grateful for your help!

Nils Rebehn

Printed in Great Britain
by Amazon

85716977R00142